Multimedia Information Retrieval

Edited by Eduardo Quevedo

Published in London, United Kingdom

IntechOpen

Supporting open minds since 2005

Multimedia Information Retrieval
http://dx.doi.org/10.5772/intechopen.83217
Edited by Eduardo Quevedo

Contributors
Lee Mariel Heucheun Yepdia, Alain Tiedeu, Zied Lachiri, Abdullah I. Al-Shoshan, Amr Adel, Brian Cusack, Eduardo Quevedo, Samuel Ortega, Martin Halicek, Himar Fabelo, Gustavo Marrero Callico, Baowei Fei, Saliha Mezzoudj, Surya Prasada Rao Borra, Appari Geetha Devi, Kalapala Vidya Sagar

First published in London, United Kingdom, 2021 by IntechOpen
IntechOpen is the global imprint of INTECHOPEN LIMITED, registered in England and Wales, registration number: 11086078, 5 Princes Gate Court, London, SW7 2QJ, United Kingdom
Printed in Croatia

British Library Cataloguing-in-Publication Data
A catalogue record for this book is available from the British Library

Additional hard and PDF copies can be obtained from orders@intechopen.com

Multimedia Information Retrieval
Edited by Eduardo Quevedo
p. cm.
Print ISBN 978-1-83880-059-8
Online ISBN 978-1-83880-060-4
eBook (PDF) ISBN 978-1-83880-540-1

For EU product safety concerns:
IN TECH d.o.o., Prolaz Marije Krucifikse Kozulić 3, 51000 Rijeka, Croatia, info@intechopen.com or visit our website at intechopen.com.

Meet the editor

Eduardo Quevedo is Assistant Professor of Biostatics and Research Methodology, Mathematics Department, University of Las Palmas de Gran Canaria (ULPGC), Spain. He is also a researcher at the Institute for Applied Microelectronics (IUMA) at the same university. Dr. Quevedo received his Ph.D. from ULPGC in 2015 and received the ULPGC Outstanding Doctoral Thesis Award in 2016. He also holds degrees in Communications Engineering (2007) and Electronics Engineering (2009) from ULPGC. He was granted a national award for the best master's thesis from the Official National Telecommunications Engineering Association in 2008. His research interests are in the fields of image and video enhancement and their related statistics in a wide range of applications.

Contents

Preface

Due to increasing globalization and the explosion of media available on the Internet, computer techniques to organize, classify, and find desired media are becoming more and more relevant. To extract semantic information from multimedia data sources, the Multimedia Information Retrieval (MMIR or MIR) technique has been applied. This evolution continues to grow, as multimedia sensors are present in diverse contexts.

MIR is a broad area covering both structural issues and intelligent content analysis and retrieval. These aspects must be integrated into a seamless whole, which involves expertise from a wide variety of fields. This book presents recent applications of MIR in content-based image retrieval and fusion, bioinformation analysis and processing, forensic multimedia retrieval techniques, and audio and music classification.

The book is organized into four sections. The first two sections include two chapters each, and the last two sections contain one chapter each. Section 1, "Content-Based Image Retrieval and Fusion," discusses the application of computer techniques to search for videos and images in large databases, as well as mechanisms to apply multiple-image fusion. Section 2, "Bioinformation Analysis and Processing," examines information extraction and processing in biomedical applications. Section 3, "Forensic Multimedia Retrieval Techniques," provides the design and test of a framework addressing the challenges of evidence collection in critical infrastructures are provided. Finally, Section 4, "Audio and Music Classification and Separation," provides a full review of classification and separation algorithms for audio and music signals.

Section 1: "Content-Based Image Retrieval and Fusion"

Chapter 1, "Towards Large-Scale Image Retrieval System Using Parallel Frameworks", highlights that the increasing use of mobile devices such as smartphones has resulted in a dramatic increase in the number of images collected every day. Consequently, this chapter introduces some fundamental theories for content-based image retrieval for large-scale databases using parallel frameworks. The main issues and basic concepts of Big Data and its technologies are discussed, moving towards modern tools including cutting-edge storage platforms.

Chapter 2 "Multiple-Image Fusion Encryption (MIFE) Using Discrete Cosine Transformation (DCT) and Pseudo Random Number Generators", proposes a new multiple-image encryption algorithm based on the spectral fusion of watermarked images and new chaotic generators. First, the discrete cosine transformation and the low-pass filter of appropriate sizes are used to combine the target watermarked images in the spectral domain in two different multiplex images. Second, each of the two images is concatenated into blocks of small size, which are mixed by changing their position following the order generated by a chaotic sequence from the Logistic-May system. Finally, the fusion of both scrambled images is achieved by a nonlinear mathematical expression based on Cramer's rule to obtain two hybrid encrypted images. Then, after the decryption step, the hidden message can be retrieved from the watermarked image without any loss.

Section 2: "Bioinformation Analysis and Processing"

Chapter 3, "Information Extraction Techniques in Hyperspectral Imaging Biomedical Applications", includes an overview of information extraction techniques for hyperspectral imaging in biomedical applications. First, it presents the background of hyperspectral imaging and the main motivations of its usage for medical applications. Second, it discusses information extraction techniques based on both light propagation models within tissue and machine-learning approaches. Third, it examines the usage of such information extraction techniques in hyperspectral imaging biomedical research applications. Finally, it discusses the main advantages and disadvantages of the most commonly used image processing approaches, along with the current challenges in HSI information extraction techniques in clinical applications.

Chapter 4, "A Hybrid Image Fusion Algorithm for Medical Applications", proposes a hybrid fusion approach for brain medical imaging based on two stages. The initial stage deals with the enhancement of a computed tomography scan image exploitation, a novel with respect to other techniques such as bar graph equalization or adaptation bar graph. In the second stage, the improved computed tomography scan image is joined to tomography image exploitation, considering fusion algorithms such as Discrete Wavelet Transform and Principal Component Analysis.

Section 3: "Forensic Multimedia Retrieval Techniques"

Chapter 5, "The Role of Penetration Testing in Forensic Multimedia Retrieval Process", proposes techniques for focusing an investigation and targeting potential case information from the vulnerability identification phase, through to the media identification phase. These techniques, oriented to critical infrastructures, are based on penetration testing. Moreover, as the main issue for the digital investigator is the vast array of media in which evidence is stored or transmitted, the chapter proposes a framework of methods flexible and adaptable to the context of an investigation.

Section 4: "Audio and Music Classification and Separation"

Chapter 6, "Classification and Separation of Audio and Music Signals", presents and discusses some algorithms for the classification and separation processes of audio and music signals. The classification algorithms are divided into three categories including approaches in the real-time, frequency domain, and time-frequency distribution. Additionally, the chapter introduces some algorithms for separation and segregation of music and audio signals, like Independent Component Analysis, pitch cancellation, and those based on artificial neural networks.

The editor would like to thank the staff at IntechOpen for the opportunity to work on this book.

Eduardo Quevedo Gutiérrez
Institute for Applied Microelectronics,
University of Las Palmas de Gran Canaria,
Las Palmas de Gran Canaria, Spain

Section 1

Content-Based Image Retrieval and Fusion

Chapter 1

Towards Large Scale Image Retrieval System Using Parallel Frameworks

Saliha Mezzoudj

Abstract

Recently, the increasing use of mobile devices, such as cameras and smartphones, has resulted in a dramatic increase in the amount of images collected every day. Therefore, retrieving and managing these large volumes of images has become a major challenge in the field of computer vision. One of the solutions for efficiently managing image databases is an Image Content Search (CBIR) system. For this, we introduce in this chapter some fundamental theories of content-based image retrieval for large scale databases using Parallel frameworks. Section 2 and Section 3 presents the basic methods of content-based image retrieval. Then, as the emphasis of this chapter, we introduce in Section 1.2 A content-based image retrieval system for large-scale images databases. After that, we briefly address Big Data, Big Data processing platforms for large scale image retrieval. In Sections 5, 6, 7, and 8. Finally, we draw a conclusion in Section 9.

Keywords: big data processing platforms, image retrieval system, big data, parallel frameworks

1. Introduction

Computer vision (also called artificial vision or digital vision) is a branch of artificial intelligence whose main goal is to allow a machine to analyze, process and understand one or more images taken by an acquisition system (example: cameras, mobile, etc.) [1]. It is used to automate the tasks that the human visual system can do: recognition, motion analysis, scene reconstruction, and image restoration [1]. In this chapter, we are interested in the recognition task, there are several specialized applications based on recognition exist, such as content image search (CBIR) and image classification systems. Image classification is an important task in the field of computer vision, and it requires the development of robust classification systems, which can improve the performance of vision systems. Indeed, most image CBIR systems have three stages:

- The first step: it is the extraction of low-level characteristics of the images (extraction of descriptors). Indeed, the use of low-level image descriptors is the core of current image classification systems.

- the searching step, in which the feature vector of a query image is computed and compared to the image feature vectors of the database. As a result, the CBIR system returns the closest images to the user [2, 3].

IntechOpen

For a long time, high calculation errands caused by calculating complexity and gigantic amount of image during indexing, and retrieving steps have been obstacles for building a CBIR systems [3, 4]. Furthermore, the conventional content-based image retrieval systems have focused on small databases of face images. Therefore, it is important to generalize and train these systems on large-scale databases [5, 6]. Therefore, in this chapter, we will present the basics of CBIR systems for large-scale databases, Big Data, Big Data processing platforms for large scale image retrieval.

2. The methods for extracting visual characteristics

The extraction of features from images is the basis of any computer vision system that does recognizing. These characteristics can contain both text (keywords; annotations, etc.), and visual characteristics (color, texture, shapes, faces, etc.). We will focus on techniques for extracting these visual features only. And for that the visual characteristics (descriptors) are classified in two categories general descriptors and specific domain descriptors [7, 8]:

2.1 General descriptors

They contain low-level descriptors that give a description of color, shape, regions, textures and movement.

Color: Color is one of the most used visual characteristics in facial recognition systems or anything like that. It is relatively robust to the complexities of the background and independently of the size and orientation of the image. The most well-known representation of color is the histogram, which denotes the frequencies of occurrence of the intensities of the three color channels. Many other representations of this characteristic exist: we speak especially of the moments of color. The mathematical basis of this approach is that each color distribution can be characterized by its color moments. Furthermore, most of the information on color is concentrated on lower order moments which are respectively: mean, standard deviation, color skewness, variance, median, etc.

Texture: A wide variety of texture descriptors have been proposed in the literature. These were traditionally divided into statistical, spectral, structural and hybrid [9] approaches. Among the most popular traditional methods are probably those based on histograms, Gabor filters [10], co-occurrence matrices [11] and models (lbp) [12]. These descriptors present various strengths and weaknesses, in particular as regards their invariance with respect to the acquisition conditions.

Shape: Over the past two decades, 2D shape descriptors have been actively used in 3D search engines and sketch-based modeling techniques. Some of the most popular 2D shape descriptors are curvature scale space (CSS) [13], SIFT [14], and SURF [15]. In fact, in the literature, 2D shape descriptors are classified into two main categories: contours and regions. Outline-based shape descriptors extract shape entities from the outline of a shape only. In contrast, region-based shape descriptors obtain shape characteristics of the entire region of a shape. In addition, hybrid techniques have also been proposed, combining techniques based on the contour and the [16] region.

Movement: Movement is related to the movement of objects in the sequence and to the movement of the camera. The latter information is provided by the capture device, while the rest is implemented by means of image processing. The set of descriptors is the following [7]: Motion Activity Descriptor (MAD), Camera Motion Descriptor (CMD), Motion Trajectory Descriptor (MTD), and Warp and Parametric Motion Descriptor (WMD and PMD).

Location: The location of items in the image is used to describe items in the spatial domain. In addition, elements can also be located in the [7] time domain: Region Locator Descriptor (RLD), Spatio Time Locator Descriptor (STLD).

3. Image classification

Image classification is an important step in the image recognition process. Indeed, many image classification techniques have been proposed to date. It is considered to be one of the main types of machine learning. Various studies have been carried out in order to choose the best technique for classifying [17] images.

3.1 What is machine learning?

It is one of the subdomains of artificial intelligence (AI) which uses a series of techniques to let computers learn, (that is, gradually improve the performance of the computer on a task specific) with data, without being explicitly programmed. Indeed, machine learning covers a vast field of tasks. Below are the types of machine learning described in this section [18]:

Supervised learning (classification): In this case, the entries are tagged by an expert, and the algorithm must learn from the tags of these entries in order to predict the class of each new entry. In other words, from a set of observations X and another set of measures Y, we seek to estimate the dependencies between X and Y.

Unsupervised learning (clustering): In this case, the entries are not labeled, no expert is available, and the algorithm must predict the class of each entry. The objective of this type of learning is to describe how the data is organized and to extract homogeneous subsets.

Semi-supervised learning: the algorithm combines labeled and unlabeled examples to generate an appropriate function or class.

Learning to learn: where the algorithm learns its own inductive bias based on previous experience.

4. A content-based image retrieval system for large-scale images databases

Indeed, the most of conventional CBIR systems are evaluated on small bases of images that fit easily in main memory, such as Caltech-101 [19], Caltech-256 [20] or PASCAL VOC [21].

Recently, the increase in images produced in different fields has enabled the acquisition and storage of a large amount of images, which offers new concepts such as Big Data, which are of huge volumes of images from a variety of sources, produced in real time and exceeding the storage capacity of a single machine. Indeed, these images are difficult to process with traditional image retrieval systems.

As digital cameras become more affordable and ubiquitous, digital images are growing exponentially on the Internet, such as ImageNet 1 [22] which consists of 14,197,122 images labeled for 21,841 classes. Indeed, this enormous quantity of images makes the task of classification of images much more complex and difficult to perform, especially since traditional processing and storage methods do not always manage to cope with this enormous quantity of images.

This challenge motivated us to develop a new image search and classification system allowing the storage, management and processing of large quantities of images (Big Data), this imposes a parallelisation of calculations to obtain results in reasonable time, and optimum precision.

Massively parallel machines are more and more available at increasingly affordable costs, such is the case with multiprocessors. This justifies our motivation to direct our research efforts in large-scale image classification towards the exploitation of such architectures with new Big Data platforms that use the performance of these machines.

5. The basics of big data

Every day, we generate trillions of bytes of data (Big Data). This data comes from everywhere: from sensors used to collect climate information, messages on social media sites, digital images and videos posted online, transactional records of online purchases and GPS signals from phones mobile, to name a few sources.

Big Data is characterized by its volume (massive data); they are also known for their variety in terms of formats and new structures, as well as a requirement in terms of speed in processing. But until now, according to our research, no software is able to handle all this data which has many types and forms and which is growing very rapidly. So Big Data issues are part of our daily life, and more advanced solutions are needed to manage this mass of data in a short time.

Distributed computing is concerned with processing large amounts of data. This processing cannot be achieved with traditional data processing paradigms, it requires the use of distributed platforms. In the literature, there are several solutions, for the implementation of this paradigm. Among these solutions we find the example Google, which has developed a very reliable programming model for the processing of Big Data: it is the MapReduce model. This model is implemented on several platforms such as the Hadoop platform. Despite all these advantages, Hadoop suffers from latency problems which is the main cause of development of a new alternative to improve the performance of processing data, it is the Spark platform which is more powerful, more flexible and faster than Hadoop MapReduce.

In this chapter, we will explain the basics of Big Data, Big Data processing platforms, as well as storage.

5.1 Definition

Big Data refers to a very large volume of often heterogeneous data which has several forms and formats (text, sensor data, sound, video, route data, log files, etc.), and including heterogeneous formats: structured data, unstructured and semi-structured. Big Data has a complex nature that requires powerful technologies and advanced algorithms for its processing and storage. Thus, it cannot be processed using tools such as the traditional DBMS [23]. Most scientists and data experts define big data with the concept of 3Vs as follows [23]:

- Velocity: Data is generated quickly and must be processed quickly to extract useful information and relevant information. For example, Wallmart (an international chain of discount retailers) generates over 2.5 petabytes (PB) of data every hour from its customers' transactions. YouTube is another good example of the fast speed of big data.

- Variety: Big data are generated from various sources distributed in multiple formats (e.g. videos, documents, commentaries, journals). Large data sets include structured and unstructured data, public or private, local or remote, shared or confidential, complete or incomplete, etc.

- Volume: it represents the amount of data generated, stored and used. The volume of data stored today is exploding, it is almost 800,000 petabytes, Twitter generates more than 7 terabytes of data every day, Facebook generates more than 10 terabytes and the data volume in 2020 can reach 40 zeta bytes (**Figure 1**) [24].

Thereafter, the three original dimensions are widened by two other dimensions of big data (also known as the "5 V Big Data"):

- Truth: Truthfulness (or validity) of data is the reliability and accuracy of data, and the confidence that big data inspires in decision-makers. If the users of this data doubt its quality or relevance, it becomes difficult to invest more in it.

- Value: This last V plays a key role in Big Data, the Big Data approach only makes sense to achieve strategic goals of creating value for customers and for companies in all areas (**Figure 2**).

One of the reasons for the emergence of the concept of Big Data is the need to realize the technical challenge of processing large volumes of information of several types (structured, semi-structured and unstructured) generated at high speed. Big Data is based on four data sources [25]:

1. The logs (connection logs) from traffic on the company's official website: These data sources are the paths taken by visitors to reach the site: search engines, directories, bounces from other sites, etc. Businesses today have a web storefront through its official website. The latter generates traffic that it is essential to analyze, so these companies have trackers on the different pages in order to measure the navigation paths, or the time spent on each page, etc. Some of the best-known analytics solutions include: Google Analytics, Adobe Omniture, Coremetics.

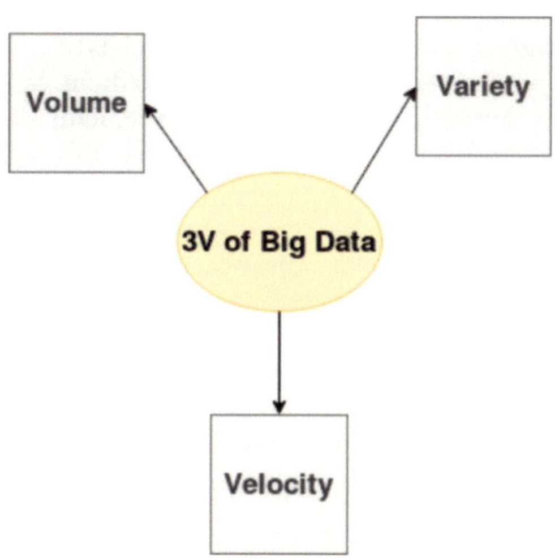

Figure 1.
The 3 V big data model.

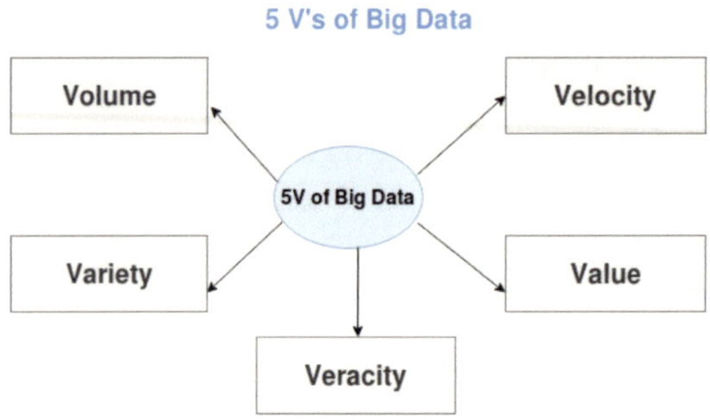

Figure 2.
The 5 V big data model.

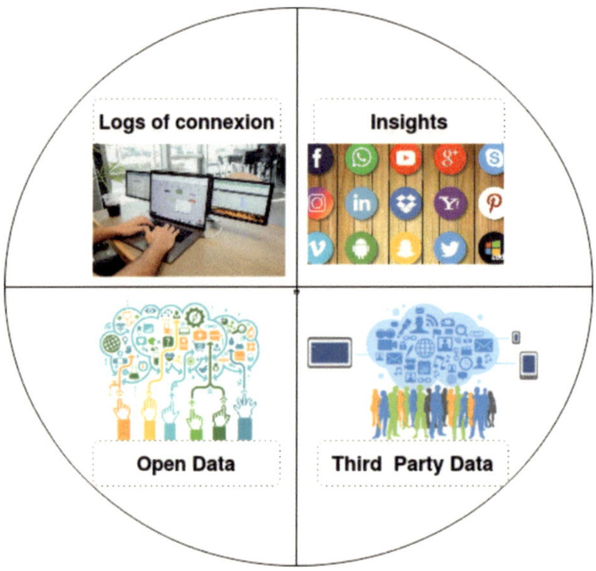

Figure 3.
The four sources of big data.

2. Social media insights: A complementary approach is to collect comments on posts and apply sentiment analysis algorithms to them. Let us mention a few avenues to follow our various accounts: Hootsuite, Radian6 or even the APIs made available and queried with the Power Query add-in for Excel, IRaMuTeQ for the analysis of textual data.

3. Behavioral data (third party data) These data are all data on Internet users collected via forms or cookies. Beyond traditional identity information (sex, age, CSP, etc.), it is now much more efficient to measure behavior (navigation, hardware configuration, time spent on pages, etc.). For this, there are specialized web players who help us collect information on our customers or prospects and thus improve communication campaigns. Some players in the field of third party data: Bluekai, Exelate, Weborama, Datalogix, etc.

4. Open and reusable data "Open data" are all open and reusable data, it makes possible to put open data online, to make the data more reliable and to make them reusable and usable, where openness consists in making the data public: free of rights, downloadable, reusable and free. The opening does not apply

to private data, sensitive and security information, documents protected by copyright, etc. (**Figure 3**).[1]

5.2 Big data processing and storage technologies

Big Data requires redefining the data storage and processing systems that can support this volume of data. Indeed, several technologies have been proposed in order to represent this data, these technologies take at least one axis between the two, either improving storage capacities or improving computing power [23]:

- Improved computing power: the goal of these techniques is to allow processing on a large set of data, at considerable cost, and to improve execution performance such as processing time and tolerance breakdowns. Before the appearance of the Hadoop platform, there were several technologies such as Could Computing, massively parallel MPP architectures and In-Memory technologies.

- Improvement of storage capacities: improvement of storage of distributed systems, where the same file can be distributed over several hard drives, this allows storage volumes to be increased by using basic hardware. These storage technologies are always evolving to offer faster access to data such as NoSQL, HDFS from the Hadoop platform, HBase, Cloud Computing, etc.

6. MapReduce

6.1 Why MapReduce?

Traditional business systems normally have a centralized server to store and process data. The traditional model is certainly not suited to handling large volumes of scalable data and cannot be handled by standard database servers. In addition, the centralized system creates too much bottleneck when processing multiple files simultaneously. Google solved this bottleneck issue using MapReduce template.

6.2 MapReduce model definition

It was designed in the 2000s by Google engineers. It is a programming model designed to process several terabytes of data on thousands of computing nodes in a [26] cluster. MapReduce can process terabytes and petabytes of data faster and more efficiently. Therefore, its popularity has grown rapidly for various brands of companies in many fields. It provides a highly efficient platform for parallel execution of applications, allocation of data in distributed database systems, and fault tolerant network communications [27]. The main goal of MapReduce is to facilitate data parallelization, distribution, and load balancing in a simple [26] library.

6.3 The MapReduce model architecture

Google created MapReduce to process large quantities unstructured or semi-structured data, such as documents and logs of requests for web pages, on large clusters of nodes. It produced different types of data, such as inverted indices or

[1] The four sources of big data, https://www.communication-web.net/2016/03/07/les-4-sources-du-big-data/

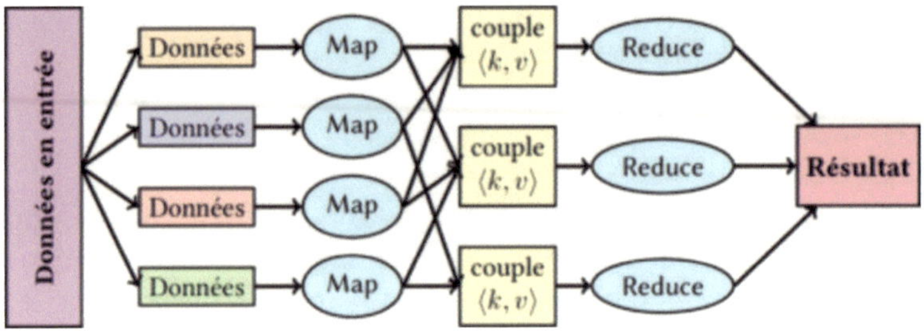

Figure 4.
An example of data flow in the MapReducee big data architecture [29].

URL access frequencies [28]. The MapReduce has three main parts, including the Master, the Map and reduce function. An example of this data flow is shown in **Figure 4**.

The Master is responsible for the management of the Map and Reduce functions and the provision of data and procedures, he organizes communication between mappers and reducers. The map function applies to each input record and produces a list of intermediate records. The Collapse function (also known as Reducer) is applied to each group of intermediate records with the same key and generates a value. Therefore, the MapReduce process includes the following steps:

- The input data are divided into records.
- Map functions process this data and produce key/value pairs for each record.
- All key/value pairs resulting from the Map function are merged together and grouped by a key, then they are sorted.
- The intermediate results are passed to the Reduce function, which will produce the final result [30].

7. Big data processing platforms

7.1 The Hadoop platform for the distributed computing of big data

First of all, Hadoop is a free framework, written in java, created and distributed by the Apache foundation, and intended for the processing of large data (of the order of petabytes and more) as well as for their intensive management. Inspired by several technical publications written by the giant Google, its goal is to provide a distributed, scalable and extensible storage and data processing system. It can handle a large number of data types (including unstructured data). We say that it is organized in a non-relational mode, it is more general than NoSQL, we can for example store data with two types of systems HDFS (Hadoop Distributed File System) and HBase which form a database management system oriented data, columns projected for servers distributed in clusters [31].

Hadoop parallelizes the processing of data across many nodes that are part of a cluster of computers, which speeds up calculations and hides the latency of input and output operations. Hadoop contains a reliable distributed file system that ensures fault tolerance through data replication.

7.2 The Spark platform for the distributed computing of big data

7.2.1 Motivation of Spark

Since its inception, Hadoop has become an important technology for Big Data. One of the main reasons for this success is its ability to manage huge amounts of data regardless of their type (structured, semi-structured, unstructured). However, users have been consistently complaining about the high latency issue with Hadoop MapReduce stating that the batch response to all of these real-time applications is very painful when it comes to processing and analysis data.

7.2.2 History of Spark

Spark is a high-speed compute cluster developed by contributions from nearly 250 developers from 50 AMPLab companies at UC Berkeley, to make data analysis faster and easier to write and thus run. Spark started in 2009 as a research project in the Berkeley Lab RAD, which would later become AMPLLab. Researchers in the lab had previously worked on Hadoop MapReduce, and observed that MapReduce was ineffective for iterative and interactive computing jobs. So from the start Spark was designed to be fast for interactive queries and iterative algorithms, bringing ideas like in-memory storage support and efficient fault recovery. Research papers have been published about Spark at academic conferences and shortly after its inception in 2009 it was already 10–100 times faster than MapReduce for some jobs. Some of the early Spark users were other groups in UC Berkeley, including researchers, such as the Millennium Mobile Project, which used Spark to monitor and forecast traffic jams in San Bay. Francisco Machine Learning. In a very short time, however, many external organizations have started using Spark.

In 2011, AMPLab started developing high-level components on Spark, such as Shark and Spark streaming. These and other components are sometimes referred to as Berkeley Data Analytics Stack (ODB). The Spark was open source in March 2010, and it was transferred to the Apache Software Foundation on June 2013, where it is now a high level [32] project.

7.2.3 Definition

Apache Spark is an open source processing framework, it is built around speed, ease of use and the ability to handle large data sets, which are of diverse nature (text data, graph data, etc.), Spark extends the MapReduce model to efficiently support multiple types of computations, including iterative processing, interactive queries, and flow processing (**Figure 5**) [32].[2]

7.2.4 Advantages of Spark over Hadoop MapReduce

Spark is a strong framework for future large data applications that may require low latency queries, iterative computing, and real-time processing. The Spark has many advantages over the Hadoop MapReduce Framework among them we find [32, 33]:

7.2.4.1 Speed

Spark is an open source compute environment similar to Hadoop, but it has some useful differences that make it superior in some workloads, it allows loading the

[2] https://meritis.fr/bigdata/larchitecture-framework-spark/

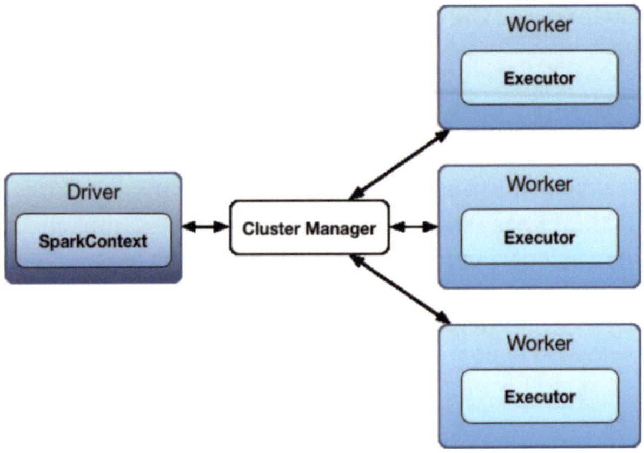

Figure 5.
Spark architecture [32].

dataset into distributed memory to optimize iterative workload and queries. Spark can run jobs 10 to 100 times faster than Hadoop MapReduce simply by reducing the number of reads and writes to disk.

7.2.4.2 Iterative processing

There are many algorithms which apply the same function to several steps. Like learning algorithms, Hadoop MapReduce is based on an acyclic data flow model, that is, the output of a previous MapReduce job is the input of the next MapReduce job. In this case we waste a lot of time in the I/O operation, so in Hadoop MapReduce between two MapReduce operations, there is a synchronization barrier and we need to keep the data on disk every time [33].

But with Spark, the concept of RDD (Resilient Distributed Datasets) allows data to be saved to memory and preserve disk only for result operations. So it does not have a whole synchronization barrier that could possibly slow down the process. So Spark allows to reduce the number of read/write on the disk.

7.2.4.3 Interactive queries

For processing in interactive data extraction algorithms where a user needs to run multiple queries on the same subset of data, Hadoop loads the same data multiple times from disk depending on the number of queries.

But Spark loads the data only once, it stores that data in distributed memory, then it does the proper processing. For processing in interactive data extraction algorithms where a user needs to run multiple queries on the same subset of data.

7.2.4.4 Richer

Spark provides concise and consistent APIs to Scala, Java and Python and Supports multiple functions (actions and transformations), unlike Hadoop, there are only two Map and Reduce functions.

7.2.4.5 Ease of use

Spark lets you quickly write applications in Java, Scala, or Python with simple, readable instructions.

7.2.4.6 General

On the general side, Spark is designed to cover a wide range of workloads that previously require separate distributed systems, including real-time processing applications, iterative algorithms, interactive queries, and streaming. By supporting these workloads in the same engine, Spark makes it easy and inexpensive to combine the different types of processing, which is often required in production data analysis pipelines.

7.2.4.7 Spark's real-time streaming method to process streams

In case of Hadoop MapReduce, it is just possible to process a flow of stored data, but with Apache Spark, it is thus possible to modify the data in real time thanks to Spark streaming [32].

7.2.4.8 Graphics processing

Developers can now as well make use of Apache Spark for graphics processing which maps relationships in data between various entities such as people and objects [32].

7.2.4.9 Learning algorithms

Spark comes with a learning library called MLlib, it provides several types of learning algorithms, including classification, regression, grouping and collaborative filtering, as well as supporting features like evaluation of the template and data import [32]. But in Hadoop you have to integrate a learning library called Mahout.

7.2.4.10 Quick management of structured data

Spark SQL is Spark's module for working with structured data, it allows querying data structured as a Distributed Data Set (RDD) in Spark, with built-in APIs in Python, Scala, and Java.[3]

7.2.4.11 Storage general

Spark uses the HDFS file system for data storage. It also works with any Hadoop compatible data source, including, HBase, Cassandra, etc.

7.2.4.12 Interactive

Offers an interactive console for Scala and Python. This is not yet available in Java.

7.2.5 Deployment

Executing heavy processing on a cluster, controlling the slave nodes, distributing the tasks for them fairly, and arbitrating the amount of CPU and memory that will be allocated to each process, this is the role of a cluster manager. Spark currently offers three solutions for this: Spark standalone, YARN and Mesos. Comes with Spark,

[3] Spark Programming Guide-Spark 1.2.0 Documentation. [Online]. Available: http://spark.apache.org/docs/1.2.0/programming-guide.html

Spark Standalone is the easiest way to set up. This cluster manager relies on Akka for exchanges and on Zookeeper to guarantee the high availability of the master node. It has a console to supervise processing, and a mechanism to collect logs from slaves.

Alternatively, YARN the Hadoop cluster manager, Spark can run on it, and alongside Hadoop jobs. Finally, more sophisticated and more general, Mesos allows you to configure more finely the allocation of resources (memory, CPU) to different applications.

7.2.6 Components of Spark

Because Spark's core engine is both fast and versatile, it powers multiple specialized high-level components for various workloads, such as SQL or machine learning. These components allow you to combine them like libraries in a software project. Spark Core: Contains the basic functionality of Spark, including components for job scheduling, memory management, disaster recovery, interaction with storage systems, and more. Spark Core is also the API that defines Elastic Distributed Datasets (RDDs), which are the main programming abstractions in Spark. RDDs represent a collection of objects distributed over several compute nodes that can be manipulated in parallel. Spark Core offers many APIs for building and manipulating these collections.

Other than Spark Core API, there are additional libraries that are part of the Spark ecosystem and provide additional capabilities in big data analysis 6. These libraries are: Spark streaming, Spark SQL, Spark MLlib, Spark GraphX (**Figure 6**) [32].

7.2.7 RDD dataset resilient distributed

7.2.7.1 Definition

An RDD is a collection of objects partitioned across a set of machines, allowing programmers to perform in-memory calculations on large clusters in a way that provides fault tolerance.[4]

7.2.7.2 Characteristics

1. RDD achieves fault tolerance through a notion of lineage: if a partition of an RDD is lost, the RDD has enough information to simply rebuild that partition. This removes the need for replication to achieve fault tolerance.

2. There are two possibilities to create an RDD either to reference external data or to parallelize an existing collection. Spark allows you to create an RDD from any data source accepted by Hadoop (local file, HDFS, HBase, etc.).

3. You can modify an RDD with a transformation, but the transformation returns you a new RDD while the original RDD remains the same.

4. RDD supports two types of operations Transformations and Actions:

Transformation: Transformations do not return a single value, they return a new RDD. Nothing is evaluated when you call a transform function. The evaluation

[4] Spark Programming Guide - Spark 1.2.0 Documentation. [Online]. Available: http://spark.apache.org/docs/1.2.0/programming-guide.html.

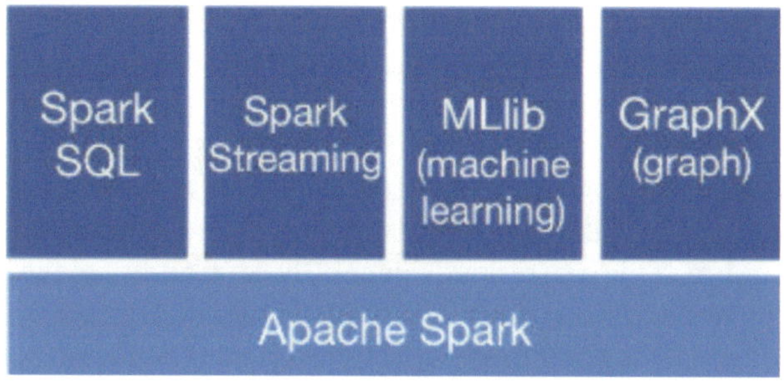

Figure 6.
Spark components [32].

of transformations is lazy, operations are performed only when a result must be returned. **Action:** an operation that evaluates and returns a new value. When an action function is called on an RDD object, all data processing requests were computed at that time and the result value is returned [33].

8. Storage

When processing a large amount of data, input data and results should be stored. Additionally, the performance of data intensive applications typically depends on the hardware and software infrastructure used for storage.

8.1 Classical storage

In this type of storage, the primary and easiest way to store data is a simple hard drive attached directly to the node. This type of storage system is sometimes referred to as a direct storage (DAS). On these disks, data is stored using a classic hierarchical file system like ext3 or ReiserFS. These file systems are typically implemented by an operating system driver as a sensitive part for security, performance, and reliability. This type of storage allows for fast read and write operations since everything is done locally. It is also simple to use as it is used with any operating system. However, there is no easy way to exchange data between multiple nodes.

8.2 Centralized network storage

A second way to store data is centralized network storage, usually referred to as etworkAttached Storage (NAS). In this case, a node has one or more disk connected and allows other nodes to read and write files through a standard interface and serve them through the network. Network File System (NFS) is primarily a protocol for accessing files over the network. While the server is free to implement any means of accessing the actual data to be provided over the network, most implementations simply depend on whether the data is directly accessible on the server. One of the main advantages of this type of architecture is the ease of sharing data between multiple compute nodes. Since the data is stored on a server, it is easily maintained.

8.3 Parallel and distributed storage

In order to overcome the limitations of centralized network storage, data can be distributed across multiple storage nodes. Using multiple nodes allows access to multiple files at the same time without conflict. It also allows better throughput to play the same file when there are replicas on multiple nodes. A distributed file system is usually designed to be better than centralized storing. Additionally, in theory, distributed storage systems can avoid the single point of the fault tolerance problem.

The distributed storage system often has a single entry point node that receives all requests to read or write data. As its role is central and critical, its work should be kept to a minimum. This master node generally only allows global collaboration among all the nodes involved in the storage system and can store metadata (file name, file size, access attributes, ...). Thus, when a request to read or write a file is received, the client is redirected to another node which will actually process his request. However, while the metadata can be stored on the master node, the actual data is still stored on other nodes and can be reproduced. The downside of distributed storage is that for the best performance, the application should consider locality. This is because even though it was thought that the default behavior of the storage system might be quite good, it is usually better to read or write data from the node closest to the system storage from'a node with a high network cost.

An example of this storage system is the Hadoop Distributed File System (HDFS) and Tachyon.

8.3.1 HDFS architecture

HDFS has a master/slave architecture. An HDFS cluster consists of a single master called NameNode which manages the namespace of the file system and regulates access to files by clients (open, close, rename, etc.), as well as a set of DataNodes to manage the actual data storage (**Figure** 7) [30].

8.4 Definition of Tachyon

Tachyon is a memory-centric, distributed storage system that allows users to share data across platforms and perform read/write actions at memory speed across cluster processing platforms. It also achieves a write rate of 110x more than in HDFS [34]. To ensure fault tolerance, the lost output is recovered by rerunning the operations that created the output, called lineage [34]. Thus, the Tachyon lineage option is seen as a major challenge in Tachyon, and the lineage layer provides high throughput I/O and follows the job sequence and data lineage in the storage layer.

8.4.1 Tachyon architecture

Indeed, Tachyon uses a standard master–slave architecture similar to HDFS (see **Figure** 8),[5] this architecture is called master-worker.

The master manages the metadata and contains a workflow manager, the latter interacts with a cluster resource manager to allocate resources and recalculate. Whereas, workers manage local resources and report status to the master, and each worker uses a RAM disk to store memory-mapped files.

8.4.2 The components of Tachyon

Tachyon's design uses a single master and multiple workers. Tachyon can be divided into three components, the master, the workers and the customers. The master and workers together constitute the Tachyon servers, which are the components that a system administrator would maintain and manage. Customers are

[5] https://www.slideshare.net/DavidGroozman/tachyon-meetup-slides

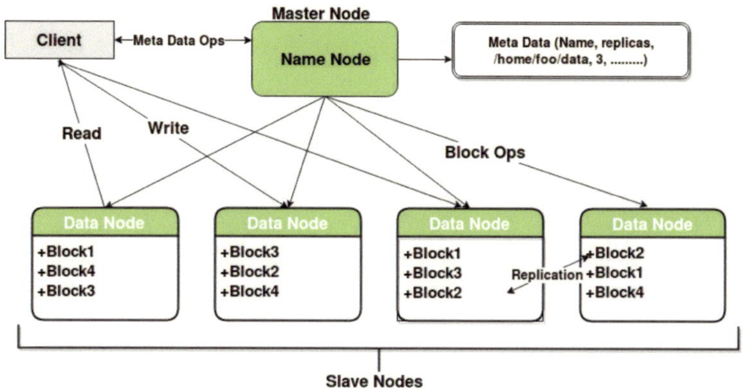

Figure 7.
HDFS architecture [30].

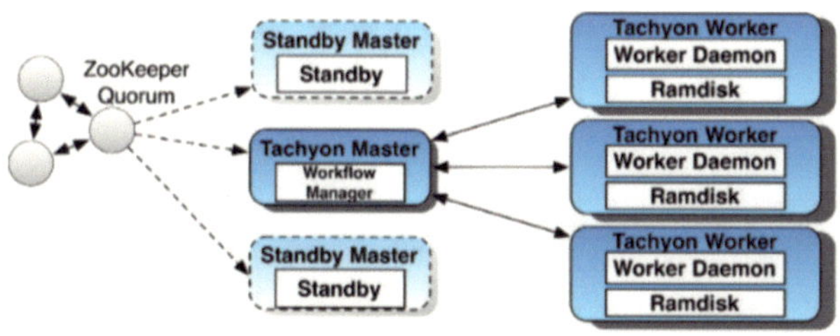

Figure 8.
The Tachyon architecture [34].

typically applications, such as Spark or MapReduce, or Tachyon command line users. So Tachyon users usually only need to interact with the client part of Tachyon [34].

a. **Master:** Tachyon can be deployed in one of two main modes, a single master or several masters. The master is primarily responsible for managing the overall metadata of the system, for example, the file system tree. Clients can interact with the master to read or modify this metadata. In addition, all workers periodically poll the master to maintain their participation in the cluster. The master does not initiate communication with the components; it only interacts with components responding to requests.

b. **Workers:** Tachyon workers are responsible for managing the local resources allocated to Tachyon. These resources could be local memory, SSD or hard drive and they are user configurable. Tachyon workers store data as blocks, and respond to customer requests to read or write data by reading or creating new blocks. However, the worker is only responsible for the data in these blocks.

c. **Customer:** The Tachyon client provides users with a gateway to interact with Tachyon servers. It initiates communication with the master to carry out metadata operations and with workers for reading and writing data.

9. Conclusion

In this chapter, we presented the domain of content based image retrieval system for large scale images using parallel platforms, we covered the basic concepts of content based image retrieval system. We introduced content based image retrieval system for large scale images (Big data) databases and its problems, the definition of Big Data and its platforms, these later allow us to go beyond classic tools, which fail to process these huge volumes of data, and move towards modern tools, which face to the large data size. Some of the tools we have introduced in this chapter include storage platforms like HDFS and Tachyon and processing platforms like Hadoop MapReduce and Spark.

Author details

Saliha Mezzoudj
Applied Mathematics Laboratory, Department of Computer Science, University of ALGER 1, Algeria

*Address all correspondence to: saliha.mezzoudj@yahoo.com

References

[1] Nicu Sebe, Ira Cohen, Ashutosh Garg, and Thomas S Huang. Machine learning in computer vision, volume 29. Springer Science & Business Media, 2005.

[2] Ricardo da Silva Torres and Alexandre X Falcao. Content-based image retrieval: Theory and applications. RITA, 13(2):161-185, 2006.

[3] Saliha Mezzoudj, Rachid Seghir, Yassmina Saadna, et al. A parallel content-based image retrieval system using spark and tachyon frameworks. *Journal of King Saud University-Computer and* Information Sciences, 2019.

[4] Chunhao Gu and Yang Gao. A content-based image retrieval system based on hadoop and lucene. In *2012 Second International Conference on Cloud and Green Computing (CGC)*, Pages 684-687. IEEE, 2012.

[5] Siyao Fu, Haibo He, and Zeng-Guang Hou. Learning race from face: A survey. IEEE Transactions on Pattern Analysis and Machine Intelligence, 36(12): 2483-2509, 2014.

[6] Mezzoudj Saliha, Behloul Ali, and Seghir Rachid. Towards large-scale face-based race classification on spark framework. Multimedia Tools and Applications, 78(18):26729-26746, 2019.

[7] Bangalore S Manjunath, Philippe Salembier, and Thomas Sikora. *Introduction to MPEG-7: Multimedia Content Description Interface*, volume 1. John Wiley & Sons, 2002.

[8] Khushboo Khurana and Reetu Awasthi. Techniques for object recognition in images and multi-object detection. *International journal of advanced research in Computer Engineering & Technology (IJARCET)*, 2(4):pp–1383, 2013.

[9] Majid Mirmehdi. *Handbook of Texture Analysis*. Imperial College Press, 2008.

[10] Francesco Bianconi and Antonio Fernández. Evaluation of the effects of gab or filter parameters on texture classification. Pattern Recognition, 40(12):3325-3335, 2007.

[11] Robert M Haralick. Statistical and structural approaches to texture. Proceedings of the IEEE, 67(5):786-804, 1979.

[12] Dong-Chen He and Li Wang. Texture unit, texture spectrum, and texture analysis. IEEE Transactions on Geoscience and Remote Sensing, 28(4):509-512, 1990.

[13] Farzin Mokhtarian, Sadegh Abbasi, and Josef Kittler. Efficient and robust retrieval by shape content through curvature scale space. In *Image Databases and Multi-Media Search*, Pages 51-58. World Scientific, 1997.

[14] David G Lowe. Distinctive image features from scale-invariant keypoints. International Journal of Computer Vision, 60(2):91-110, 2004.

[15] Herbert Bay, Tinne Tuytelaars, and Luc Van Gool. Surf: Speeded up robust features. In *European conference on computer vision*, Pages 404-417. Springer, 2006.

[16] Wong, Ooi Qun and Rajendran, Parvathy. Image Segmentation using Modified Region-Based Active Contour Model. J. Eng. Appl. Sci. 2019;14:5710-5718

[17] Maneela Jain and Pushpendra Singh Tomar. Review of image classification methods and techniques. *International journal of engineering research and technology*, 2(8), 2013.

[18] W Chao. Machine Learning Tutorial. *National Taiwan University*, 2011.

[19] Jean Ponce, Tamara L Berg, Mark Everingham, David A Forsyth, Martial Hebert, Svetlana Lazebnik, Marcin Marszalek, Cordelia Schmid, Bryan C Russell, Antonio Torralba, et al. Dataset issues in object recognition. In *Toward category-level object recognition*, pages 29-48. Springer, 2006.

[20] Gregory Griffin, Alex Holub, and Pietro Perona. Caltech-256 Object Category Dataset. 2007.

[21] Mark Everingham, Luc Van Gool, Christopher KI Williams, John Winn, and Andrew Zisserman. The pascal visual object classes (voc) challenge. International Journal of Computer Vision, 88(2):303-338, 2010.

[22] Olga Russakovsky, Jia Deng, Hao Su, Jonathan Krause, Sanjeev Satheesh, Sean Ma, Zhiheng Huang, Andrej Karpathy, Aditya Khosla, Michael Bernstein, et al. Imagenet large scale visual recognition challenge. International Journal of Computer Vision, 115(3):211-252, 2015.

[23] Ahmed Oussous, Fatima-Zahra Benjelloun, Ayoub Ait Lahcen, and Samir Belfkih. Big data technologies: A survey. *Journal of King Saud University-Computer and* Information Sciences, 30(4):431-448, 2018.

[24] Raghavendra Kune, Pramod Kumar Konugurthi, Arun Agarwal, Raghavendra Rao Chillarige, and Rajkumar Buyya. The anatomy of big data computing. Software: Practice and Experience, 46(1):79-105, 2016.

[25] Desamparados Blazquez and Josep Domenech. Big data sources and methods for social and economic analyses. Technological Forecasting and Social Change, 130:99-113, 2018.

[26] Alberto Fernández, Sara del Río, Abdullah Bawakid, and Francisco Herrera. Fuzzy rule based classification systems for big data with mapreduce: Granularity analysis. Advances in Data Analysis and Classification, 11(4): 711-730, 2017.

[27] Lu Lu, Xuanhua Shi, Hai Jin, Qiuyue Wang, Daxing Yuan, and Song Wu. Morpho: A decoupled mapreduce framework for elastic cloud computing. Future Generation Computer Systems, 36:80-90, 2014.

[28] Seyed Nima Khezr and Nima Jafari Navimipour. Mapreduce and its applications, challenges, and architecture: A comprehensive review and directions for future research. Journal of Grid Computing, 15(3): 295-321, 2017.

[29] Jeffrey Dean and Sanjay Ghemawat. Mapreduce: Simplified data processing on large clusters. Communications of the ACM, 51(1):107-113, 2008.

[30] Vignesh Prajapati. *Big Data Analytics with R and Hadoop*. Packt Publishing Ltd, 2013.

[31] Aditya B Patel, Manashvi Birla, and Ushma Nair. Addressing big data problem using hadoop and map reduce. In *2012 Nirma University International Conference on Engineering (NUiCONE)*, Pages 1-5. IEEE, 2012.

[32] Holden Karau, Andy Konwinski, Patrick Wendell, and Matei Zaharia. *Learning spark: lightning-fast big data analysis*. " O'Reilly Media, Inc.", 2015.

[33] Matei Zaharia, Mosharaf Chowdhury, Michael J Franklin, Scott Shenker, and Ion Stoica. Spark: Cluster computing with working sets. HotCloud, 10(10-10):95, 2010.

[34] Haoyuan Li, Ali Ghodsi, Matei Zaharia, Scott Shenker, and Ion Stoica. Tachyon: Reliable, memory speed storage for cluster computing frameworks. In *Proceedings of the ACM Symposium on Cloud Computing*, Pages 1-15. ACM, 2014.

Chapter 2

Multiple-Image Fusion Encryption (MIFE) Using Discrete Cosine Transformation (DCT) and Pseudo Random Number Generators

Lee Mariel Heucheun Yepdia, Alain Tiedeu and Zied Lachiri

Abstract

This chapter proposes a new multiple-image encryption algorithm based on spectral fusion of watermarked images and new chaotic generators. Logistic-May (LM), May-Gaussian (MG), and Gaussian-Gompertz (GG) were used as chaotic generators for their good properties in order to correct the flaws of 1D chaotic maps (Logistic, May, Gaussian, Gompertz) when used individually. Firstly, the discrete cosine transformation (DCT) and the low-pass filter of appropriate sizes are used to combine the target watermarked images in the spectral domain in two different multiplex images. Secondly, each of the two images is concatenated into blocks of small size, which are mixed by changing their position following the order generated by a chaotic sequence from the Logistic-May system (LM). Finally, the fusion of both scrambled images is achieved by a nonlinear mathematical expression based on Cramer's rule to obtain two hybrid encrypted images. Then, after the decryption step, the hidden message can be retrieved from the watermarked image without any loss. The security analysis and experimental simulations confirmed that the proposed algorithm has a good encryption performance; it can encrypt a large number of images combined with text, of different types while maintaining a reduced Mean Square Error (MSE) after decryption.

Keywords: spectral fusion, chaotic generators, image encryption, watermarked images

1. Introduction

Several image encryption algorithms are being developed today to meet privacy needs in multimedia communications [1–33]. With the rapid expansion of the Internet, innovative technologies, and cryptanalysis, it has become necessary to build new and appropriate cryptosystems for secured data transfer, especially for digital images. Nowadays, a large quantity of images is produced in various fields and exchanged sometimes with text through different channels, favoring the development of multiple-image encryption (MIE) instead of single-image encryption (SIE). A secure technique to protect the large amounts of data (image and text) exchanged in unsecured communication channels is to combine cryptography and watermarking [26, 27]. These two combined approaches help to produce a two-level security of the text and image, especially when the message is hidden in the image to be encrypted. Various watermarking techniques are proposed in the literature [28–32], and the most used are discrete wavelet transformation (DWT) and discrete cosine transformation (DCT). For instance, if an information, such as a signature, a logo, or a text is embedded in low- or medium-frequency DCT coefficients, then it may be recovered without any loss; however, only high-frequency DCT coefficients are lost in low-pass filtering.

In literature, many encryption algorithms, such as International Data Encryption Algorithm (IDEA), Advanced Encryption Standard (AES), and Data Encryption Standard (DES) have been proposed [1]. However, these standard algorithms do not seem to be appropriate for image encryption, because of the intrinsic features of images, such as huge data capacity, high redundancy, strong correlation among adjacent pixels, and low entropy [2]. Some basic properties of chaotic systems such as the sensitivity to the initial condition and control parameters, sensitivity to plain text, ergodicity and randomness behavior, meet the requirements for a good cryptosystem. Consequently, several cryptosystems were developed by researchers, based on chaotic systems because the latter provided a good combination of speed, high security, complexity, reasonable computational overheads, and computational power [3]. With these features, chaotic-based cryptosystems have excellent properties of confusion and diffusion, which are desirable in cryptography. Therefore, many techniques involving different chaotic systems have been published [2–12, 23], and we can distinguish one-dimensional (1D) chaotic maps and high-dimensional (HD) chaotic maps.

Among the chaotic encryption algorithms developed, the ones using a one-dimensional (1D) chaotic system like Logistic, May, Tent, and Sine map have proven to have some strengths, such as: high-level efficiency, simplicity, and high-speed encryption. 1D chaotic structures have been widely used [4] due to their simple structures, as opposed to the complex ones of higher dimensional chaotic system (which causes a relative slowness in computation). However, some schemes using the 1D map have been broken due to their weaknesses like nonuniform data output, small key space, periodic data output, and poor ergodicity properties for some ranges of control parameters [5, 6]. To overcome this drawback, some researchers stated that the 1D chaotic map should not be used alone [7, 8]. Others proposed new 1D chaotic systems with better properties like Spatiotemporal chaos in [9], coupled with the 1D chaotic map [6], the Nonlinear Chaotic map Algorithm (NCA) [10], and, more recently, nonlinear combinations of two different 1D chaotic maps [3, 11, 12]. For example, Abanda and Tiedeu [3] combined outputs of Duffing and Colpitts chaotic systems to encrypt gray and color images. Kamdeu and Tiedeu [11] proposed a fast and secured encryption scheme using new 1D chaotic systems obtained from Logistic, May, Gaussian, and Gompertz maps. In [12], Chenaghlu et al. proposed a polynomial combination of 1D chaotic maps for image encryption using dynamic functions generation.

Recently, in order to increase the efficiency of cryptosystems for multiple images, some authors proposed algorithms integrating the concept of fusion or mixing images as a step in the encryption process. Image fusion has been proven to have potential for encryption in both spatial and frequency domains. In the last 8 years, much effort has been devoted to compressing and encrypting images at the same time [13], which is considered as a new tool used to reduce the amount of data to be transmitted and protecting the use of these data against unauthorized access. In particular, the discrete cosine transformation (DCT) is employed as a useful tool for spectral fusion in most of these methods. The widely used application DCT for image compression is mainly based on its energy compaction property, which means that the low-frequency coefficients are located around the top-left corner of its spectral plane [24]. In 2018, Jridi and Alfalou [14] proposed a cryptosystem to improve a Simultaneous Fusion, Compression and Encryption (SFCE) scheme [15] in terms of time consumption, bandwidth occupation, and encryption robustness. In [16], Dongfeng et al. proposed a new scheme for simultaneous fusion, imaging and encryption of multiple target images using a single-pixel detector. This algorithm achieves good performance in terms of robustness as the number of images to multiplex increases, but suffered from reduced key space and poor quality of images recovered. Mehra and Nishchal [17] proposed an image fusion encryption based on wavelets for securing multiple images through asymmetric keys. It offers a large key space, which enhances the security of the system. In 2016, Qin et al. [18] proposed an optical multiple-image encryption scheme in diffractive imaging using spectral fusion and nonlinear operations.

More recently, Zhang and Wang [19, 20] proposed two schemes of multiple-image encryption (MIE): the first algorithm based on mixed image element and permutation, and the second MIE algorithm based on mixed image element and chaos. The cryptosystem shows good performances, but can be improved in terms of compression to reduce the size of the multiplex big image when the number of target images increases. In [21], Zhu and Zhang proposed an encryption algorithm of mixed image element based on an elliptic curve cryptosystem. Experimental results and theoretical analysis show that the algorithm possesses a large key space and can accomplish a high level of security concerning information interaction on the network platform, but the encryption and decryption computational time is long. In 2013, Abdalla and Tamimi [22] proposed a cryptosystem, which combines two or more images of different types and sizes by using a shuffling-substitution procedure. Here, the process of mixing image combines stream cipher with block cipher, on the byte level.

After analyzing most MIE algorithms operating in the spectral domain, the robustness of the cryptosystem increases with the number of input images. Consequently, the quality of decrypted images is degraded. Therefore, it is important to design cryptosystems that can keep a good compromise between a large number of images added to text to encrypt, a small MSE after decryption, and a good performance in terms of robustness and efficiency.

As a result, this chapter suggests a new MIE algorithm based on the spectral fusion of different types of watermarked images of same size using discrete cosine transformation (DCT) associated with a low-pass filter and chaotic maps. The proposed scheme has several strengths: it is robust, combines watermarking and cryptography, which produce a two-level security, uses chaotic maps with good properties, encrypts a large number of watermarked images into two hybrid ciphered images, and the quality of the reconstructed images and text is good (reduced MSE). The encryption process comprises three main steps: in the first step, target images are fused into two images through DCT and low-pass filter; in the second step, the small blocks with the size of (4×4) images are permuted in a certain order; and in the last step, which is the diffusion phase, the two scrambled images are fused by a nonlinear mathematical expression based on Cramer's rule to obtain two hybrid encrypted images. The key generation of the cryptosystem is made dependent on the plain images.

The rest of the chapter is organized as follows: Section 2 presents an overview of chaotic generators used in the cryptosystem and the description of the watermarking process. In Section 3, spectral fusion of plain images is detailed. The proposed encryption/decryption scheme is given in Section 4. In Section 5, experimental results and algorithm analyses are presented, then compared with others in the literature. We end with a conclusion in Section 6.

2. Brief review on 1D chaotic systems used

2.1 1D logistic, May, Gaussian, and Gompertz maps

The equations of 1D Logistic, May, Gaussian, and Gompertz maps are described from Eqs. (1) to (4), respectively [11].

2.1.1 1D logistic map

$$x_{n+1} = rx_n(1 - x_n) \tag{1}$$

where $x_n \in [0, 1]$ is the discrete state of the output chaotic sequence and r is the control parameter with values in the range (0, 4]. The chaotic behavior of the Logistic map is observed in the range [3.5, 4].

2.1.2 May map

$$x_{n+1} = x_n \exp\left(a(1 - x_n)\right) \tag{2}$$

where $x_n \in [0, 10.9]$ and the control parameter a belongs to the range [0, 5].

2.1.3 Gaussian map

$$x_{n+1} = \exp\left(-\alpha x_n^2\right) + c \tag{3}$$

where $\alpha \in [4.7, 17]$, $c \in [-1, 1]$.

2.1.4 Gompertz map

$$x_{n+1} = -bx_n \ln x_n \tag{4}$$

where the control parameter $b \in (0, e]$, e = 2.71829 ... and is the exponential function.

2.2 Combination of new 1D chaotic maps

The chaotic properties of 1D Logistic, May, Gaussian, and Gompertz maps are not suitable to build a secure cryptosystem when they are used alone. To solve this problem, Zhou et al. [23] proposed to combine the different seed maps. **Figure 1** shows the new map obtained from a nonlinear combination of two different 1D chaotic maps.

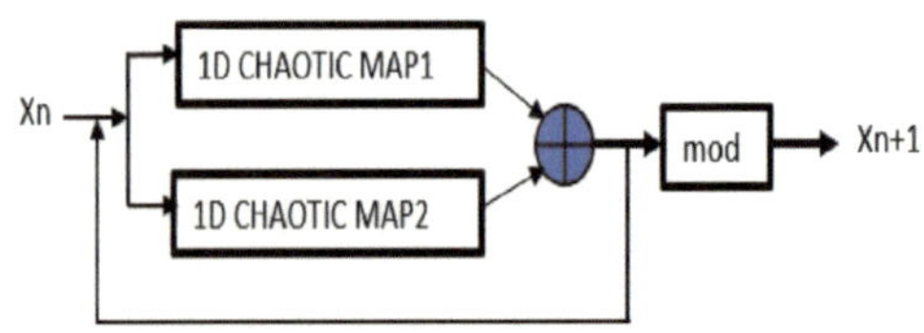

Figure 1.
New chaotic scheme.

2.2.1 Logistic-May map (LM)

Its equation is defined by Eq. (5)

$$x_{n+1} = (x_n \exp((r+9)(1-x_n)) - (r+5)x_n(1-x_n))\text{mod}2 \tag{5}$$

where $x_n \in [0,1]$ and $r \in [0,5]$. From its bifurcation diagram, we can observe that chaotic properties are excellent within [0, 5], with a maximum Lyaponuv exponent equal to 8.3.

2.2.2 May-Gaussian (MG)

Eq. (6) defines the May-Gaussian (MG) map

$$x_{n+1} = \left(x_n \exp((r+10)(1-x_n)) + \frac{(r+5)}{4} + \exp\left(-\alpha x_n^2\right)\right)\text{mod}2 \tag{6}$$

where $x_n \in [0,1]$, $r \in [0,5]$, $\alpha \in [4.7,17]$. From its bifurcation diagram, the Lyaponuv exponents are positive and belong to the range [2.5, 5.6].

2.2.3 Gaussian-Gompertz

It is defined by Eq. (7)

$$x_{n+1} = \left(\frac{(r/5+26)}{4} + \exp\left(-\alpha x_n^2\right) - (r/5+26)x_n \log x_n\right)\text{mod}2 \tag{7}$$

where $x_n \in [0,1]$, $r \in [0,5]$, $\alpha \in [4.7,17]$. It has a mean Lyaponuv exponent around 2.5.

Figure 2 illustrates the bifurcation diagram and the Lyaponuv exponent graphics of these maps. Referring to **Figure 2**, all the previous 1D chaotic systems present a wider chaotic range and a more uniform distribution of their density functions. Furthermore, the maximum Lyaponuv exponent values obtained are respectively 8.1, 5.6, and 2.5. Then, these combined 1D systems are more suitable for secure and high-speed encryption if the encryption algorithm is built around a good algebraic structure. Additively, in order to confirm the good performance of the previous pseudo random number generators, we performed the NIST statistical tests. Analysis of these results (see **Table 1**) showed that all the 15 tests were congruent for the three chaotic maps.

2.3 Description of the watermarked process

Before multiplexing the target images, a binary information in the form of a logo was inserted in one of the target images. To do this, we used a simple watermarked algorithm, which makes the hidden message imperceptible in the watermarked image. Taking advantage of the benefits of DCT, it is possible to embed an information or watermark (text, logo, image) in low- or medium-frequency DCT coefficients. In fact, DCT decomposes an image into three frequency regions: low, medium, and high frequencies. It is recommended to insert the watermark in the low- and medium-frequency regions of the host image in order to ensure imperceptibility [32]. In this work, we adopted the watermarking technique

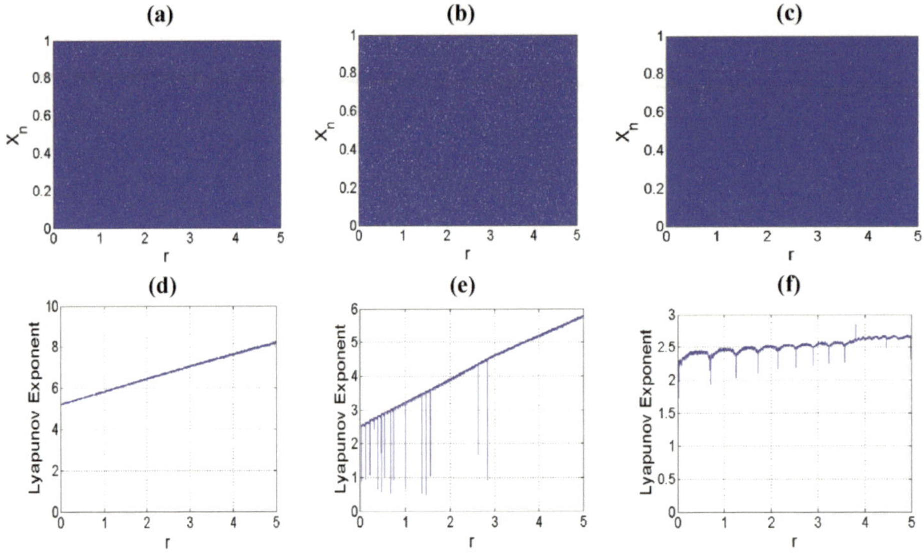

Figure 2.
Bifurcation diagrams and Lyaponuv exponent graphics of combined chaotic maps, (a) and (d) logistic-may, (b) and (e) May-Gaussian, (c) and (f) Gaussian-Gompertz.

Statistical test	Logistic-May map (LM)		May-Gaussian map (MG)		Gaussian-Gompertz map	
	p-Value	Result	p-Value	Result	p-Value	Result
Frequency	0.98147	98/100	0.99680	100/100	0.99438	100/100
Block-frequency	0.6929	97/100	0.69842	98/100	0.678415	97/100
Cumulative-sums	0.78621	96/100	0.87124	97/100	0.9014	100/100
Runs	0.88052	99/100	0.92735	100/100	0.87246	98/100
Longest-runs	0.98654	99/100	0.99815	100/100	0.97729	98/100
Rank	0.54702	97/100	0.57914	98/100	0.5873	99/100
FFT	0.87531	97/100	0.89678	98/100	0.82670	98/100
Nonoverlapping-templates	0.78951	100/100	0.75091	99/100	0.77856	98/100
Overlapping-templates	0.28435	99/100	0.18942	97/100	0.25167	98/100
Universal	0.38277	99/100	0.34834	98/100	0.37051	100/100
Approximate entropy	0.45393	98/100	0.49357	99/100	0.41560	98/100
Random-excursions	0.195257	60/60	0.192410	59/60	0.19478	59/60
Random-excursions Variant	0.14358	58/60	0.13871	57/60	0.15120	59/60
Serial	0.42962	97/100	0.47359	99/100	0.41757	97/100
Linear-complexity	0.08945	98/100	0.32876	100/100	0.15762	98/100
Final result		success		success		success

Table 1.
Statistical NIST tests results of 1,000,000 bits.

described in [33] in which the message to hide is added to the medium-frequency region discrete cosine coefficients in selected pixel blocks of size 8×8. All the blocks satisfying the condition $Ds > Av \times \alpha$ are eligible blocks suitable for watermark embedding, where Av is the average for all pixels in the block considered from

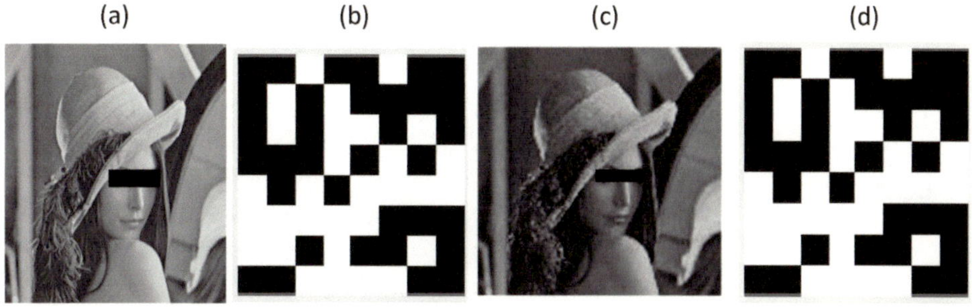

Figure 3.
Results of the watermarked process. (a) Host image (512 ×512), (b) watermark (64 ×64), (c) watermarked image, (d) recovered watermark.

the host image; *Ds* represents the difference sum for all the pixels used in the block; and α is a constant threshold value selected. The value of α must be high to ensure the most hidden message imperceptibility in the watermarked image; $\alpha \epsilon$ [0, 255].

To illustrate an embedded process, as can be seen in **Figure 3**, we used a host image of size 512×512, and a binary watermarked image of size 64×64. We can notice from **Figure 3** that the binary image (watermarked) is recovered without loss of information.

In order to protect the watermarked and host image from unauthorized access and noise attack, the watermarked image was encrypted with other images in a mixed process.

2.4 Spectral fusion of target images

In this section, N target images of size (M, M) are combined into two images, each containing $\{N/2\}$ target images. As described in [24], discrete cosine transformation (DCT) is first applied separately to each of the target images. In the second step, every spectrum is multiplied by a low-pass filter, of size (*M'*, *M'*) pixels, as indicated in **Figure 4**. In this manner, it is possible to reconstruct every target image through the relevant information contained in each block. At this step, the compression rate C_p is:

$$C_\mathrm{p} = 1\text{–}(\textit{size of multiplexed DCT spectral plane/size of N inputs images})$$

$$c_p = 1 - \left(M^2/N \times M^2\right) = 1 - 1/N \tag{8}$$

Then, after all of these target images are grouped together by a way of simple addition, the inverse discrete cosine transformation (IDCT) of the multiplex image

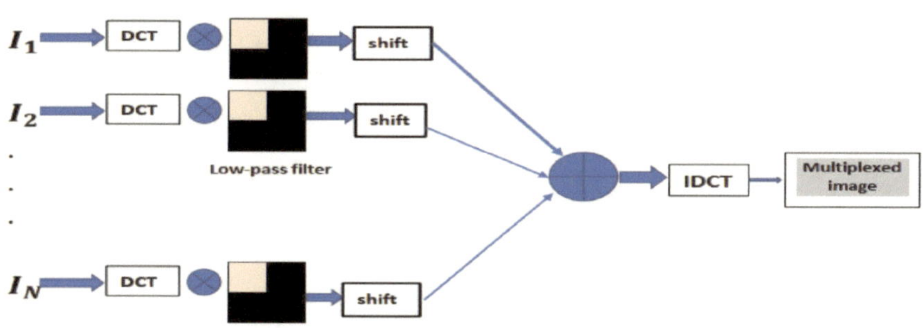

Figure 4.
Spectral fusion of target images.

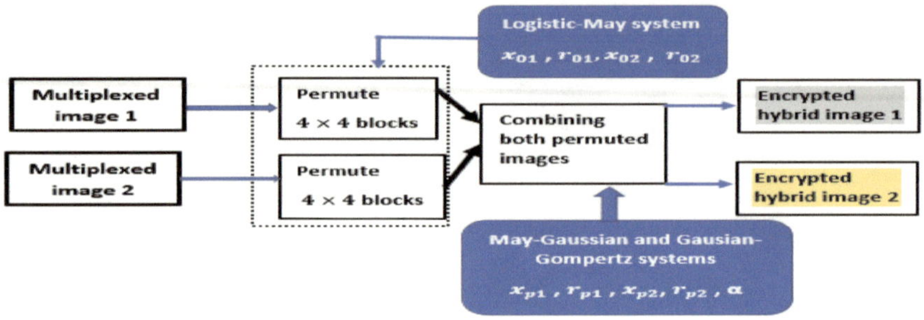

Figure 5.
Encryption scheme.

is performed. A simple rotation is performed on each of these blocks before spectral multiplexing, to prevent from information overlap. **Figure 4** illustrates the description of the process. It is possible to multiplex a large number of target images by selecting a smaller size of the filter. However, in this case, the recovered images will be highly altered. To keep a good quality of reconstructed images while maintaining a large number of target images to encrypt, we chose to group these images in two multiplex images of the same size.

2.5 Proposed encryption/decryption scheme

This section presents the proposed cryptosystem, which comprises blocks-permutation and diffusion steps using chaotic generators. **Figure 5** illustrates the entire process.

2.5.1 Encryption process

A. Blocks-permutation

The plain image is each of the two multiplex images obtained in Section 3. The plain image is decomposed into small blocks of the same size; let us choose blocks size of (4 × 4) pixels. In fact, increasing the number of blocks by using smaller block size resulted in a lower correlation and higher entropy; then, the intelligible information contained in the image will be reduced.

The permutation of blocks is realized as follows:

1. Divide the plain image I I of size $M \times M$ into k blocks of size (4×4), with $k = \frac{M}{4} \times \frac{M}{4}$

2. Use initial condition and control parameters x_{01}, r_{01} of Logistic-May system to generate a chaotic sequence by iterating k times Eq. (5). The values of the sequence X obtained are ranged in a row vector P of size $(1, k)$.

3. Repeat step 2 to generate a new sequence, using new initial condition and control parameters x_{02} and r_{02}. This second sequence is to permute the small blocks of the second multiplex image.

4. Sort the chaotic sequence P in ascending order, and get a new sequence $P' = \{P'_t\}_k = \{P'_{t1}; P'_{t2}, \ldots P'_{tk}\}$. Therefore, the sequence $x_{01}, r_{01}, x_{02}, r_{02}$ is the permutation of the sequence 1, 2, … , k.

Number all the blocks of the plain image obtained in step 1, and adjust their positions with the previous permutation of step 3. Then, the image obtained is a block image permuted.

The values x_{01}, r_{01}, x_{02}, r_{02} are calculated through Eqs. (9) and (10). In this process, we subdivide each multiplex image I_i, $(i = 1, 2)$ in two parts, P_1 and P_2 of same size.

$$x_{0i} = (x_0 + mean(I_i)/255)\text{mod}1 \tag{9}$$

$$r_{0i} = \left(r_0 + 0.1 \times \max\left(S_1, S_2\right)/N \times M \times 2^9 \right. \tag{10}$$

where, S_1 is the sum of pixels' intensities of the first part P_1 of the multiplex image I_i, and S_2 for P_2. $x_0 \in [0, 0.9]$, $r \in [0, 4.9]$.

B. Diffusion of the scrambled images

At this level, the two scrambled images are combined in order to create the final hybrid encrypted images that would be difficult to crack. The May-Gaussian and Gaussian-Gompertz systems in Eqs. (6) and (7) are used as pseudo random generators to generate two chaotic sequences after 2 M × 2 M iterations. These values are arranged in two arrays *W* and *T* of sizes 2 M × 2 M, respectively, where M represents the number of rows and columns of each scrambled image. W and *T* are converted into real values in unit 8 format; *(W = uint8(W×255); T = uint8(T×255)).* The initial conditions and control parameters of the two pseudo random numbers generators are x_{p1}, r_{p1} and x_{p2}, r_{p2}, α, respectively, for May-Gaussian and Gaussian-Gompertz systems. These parameters are determined with Eqs. (11) and (12).

$$x_{pi} = x_0 + 0.1 \times \min\left(I_i\right)/256 \tag{11}$$

$$r_{pi} = r + 0.1 \times \min\left(I_i + 1\right)/\max\left(I_i + 2\right) \tag{12}$$

where *max* (I_i) and *min* (I_i) are, respectively, maximum and minimum pixel's intensities values of I_i. $x_0 \in [0, 0.9]$, $r \in (0, 4.9]$.

$$W = \begin{pmatrix} w_{11} & w_{12} \\ w_{21} & w_{22} \end{pmatrix} \;;\; T = \begin{pmatrix} t_{11} & t_{12} \\ t_{21} & t_{22} \end{pmatrix} \tag{13}$$

The arrays *W* and *T* are divided into four sub-blocks of same size M × M. The two scrambled images $\boldsymbol{I_1}$ and $\boldsymbol{I_2}$ are linearly combined with the sub-blocks of *W* and *T* using the following equations:

$$C_1(i,j) = [w_{11} \times I_1(i,j) + w_{12} \times I_2(i,j))\text{mod}256 \oplus floor(t_{11} \times t_{21}) \times 10^{15})] \tag{14}$$

$$C_2(i,j) = [w_{21} \times I_1(i,j) + w_{22} \times I_2(i,j))\text{mod}256 \oplus floor(t_{12} \times t_{22}) \times 10^{15})] \tag{15}$$

where $C_1(i,j)$ and $C_2(i,j)$ are the two encrypted hybrid images of the cryptosystem, and ⊕ is the bit wise XOR operator. The mixed product $t_{ij} \times t_{ji}$ in the above relations enhances the quality of the merged images.

2.5.2 Decryption process

In the decryption process, the encrypted images are first decomposed using Cramer's rule in order to recover the scrambled images. Knowing the fusion keys

$(x_{p1}, r_{p1}, x_{p2}, r_{p2}, \alpha)$, the receiver can get the images I_1 and I_2 by solving the system of equations below:

$$\begin{cases} (I_1[i,j] \times w_{11} + I_2[i,j] \times w_{12})_{mod256} = C_1\left(floor(t_{11} \times t_{21}) \times 10^{15}\right) \\ (I_1[i,j] \times w_{21} + I_2[i,j] \times w_{22})_{mod256} = C_2\left(floor(t_{12} \times t_{22}) \times 10^{15}\right) \end{cases} \quad (16)$$

Then, the two multiplex images can be obtained easily by decrypting $\boldsymbol{I_1}$ and $\boldsymbol{I_2}$ through reverse permutation operations.

3. Experimental results and algorithm analysis

Numerical simulation experiments have been carried out to verify the proposed encryption method using MATLAB 2016 b platform on a PC with Core (TM) i7-353U processor of 2.5GHz. We first take eight images with 512 × 512 pixels and 256 gray levels as the target images to be encrypted, which are combined in two multiplex images as shown in **Figure 6** (*a–h*), respectively. The compression ratio C_p is 0.75 for each multiplex image. The size of low-pass filter is $(M', M') = (256, 256)$ pixels. Results are analyzed more in terms of statistical attack, differential

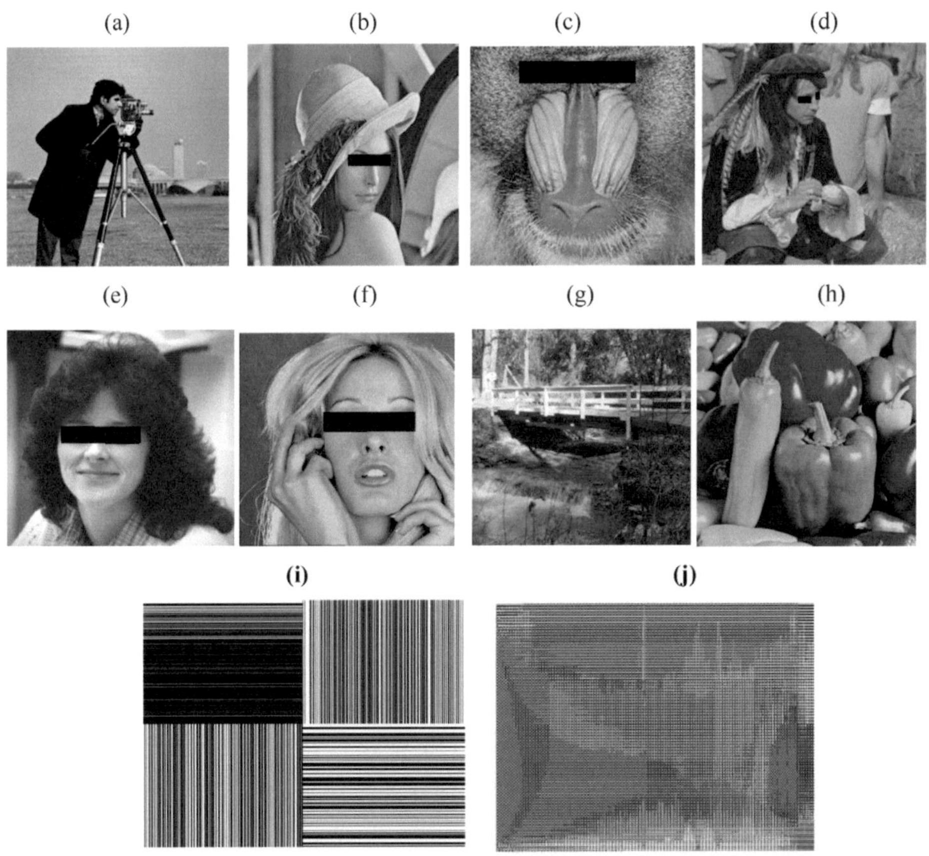

Figure 6.
Plain and combined images. (a–d) Images combined in multiplex image 1, (e–h) images combined in multiplex image 2, (i) multiplex image 1 before IDCT, (j) multiplex image 1 after IDCT.

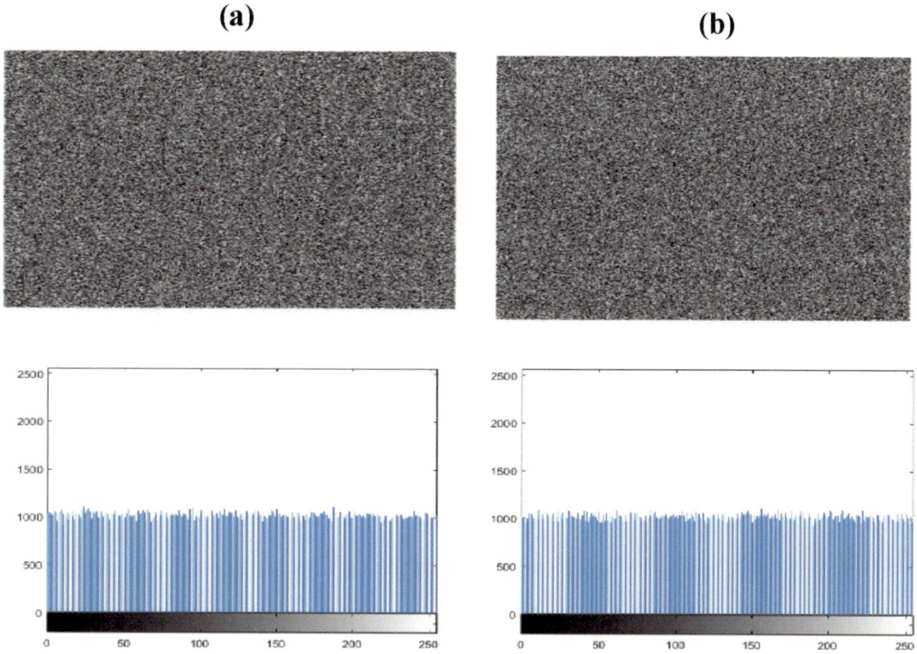

Figure 7.
Encrypted images and their histograms. (a) Multiplexed image 1, (b) multiplexed image 2.

attack, quality of decrypted images, and speed. We chose the different values as keys of the proposed cryptosystem:

x_{01} = 0.351482953177765; x_{02} = 0.972970074275508; r_{01} = 4.988242173292221; r_{02} = 4.909240772131021; x_{p1} = 0.363606938668312; x_{p2} = 0.890363879273465; r_{p1} = 4.841585120587438; r_{p2} = 4.738149127386060; α = 6.187.

The size of the filter (*M'*, *M'*) and the number of target images *N* constitute additional parameters of the key.

3.1 Statistical analysis

3.1.1 Histogram

For a well-ciphered image, all the frequencies of pixels must be uniformly distributed. As one can see in **Figure 7**, the histogram of the multiplex encrypted images is uniform.

$$NPCR = \frac{\sum_{i,j} D(i,j)}{W \times H} \times 100\% \quad (17)$$

$$UACI = \frac{1}{W \times H}\left[\sum_{i,j}\left|\frac{C_1(i,j) - C_2(i,j)|}{255}\right|\right] \times 100\% \quad (18)$$

3.1.2 Correlation analysis

A good cryptosystem produces a cipher image with a correlation coefficient close to zero, for two adjacent pixels. Five thousand pairs of adjacent pixels were chosen to calculate the correlation coefficients in horizontal, vertical, and diagonal directions respectively, by using Eq. (17).

$$C_{rxy} = \frac{K \times \sum_{i=1}^{K} X_i Y_i - \sum_{i=1}^{K} X_i^2 \times \sum_{i=1}^{K} {Y_i}^2}{\sqrt{\left(K \times \sum_{i=1}^{K} (X_i)^2 - \left(\sum_{i=1}^{K} X_i\right)^2\right) \times \left(K \times \sum_{i=1}^{K} (Y_i)^2 - \left(\sum_{i=1}^{K} Y_i\right)^2\right)}} \tag{19}$$

where X and Y are the values of two adjacent pixels in the image, C_{rxy} belongs to the range $[-1, 1]$ and K denotes the number of pairs of pixels randomly selected. C_{rxy} tends to be 1 or -1 for strong correlation and tends to be 0 for every poor correlation. **Table 2** shows the calculated correlation coefficient of 512×512 cameraman and peppers images in every direction. A mean value of the proposed encryption algorithm is about 0.0032, which tends to be zero, which is the expected value. The same result can be confirmed in **Figure 8**, where the pixels of encrypted

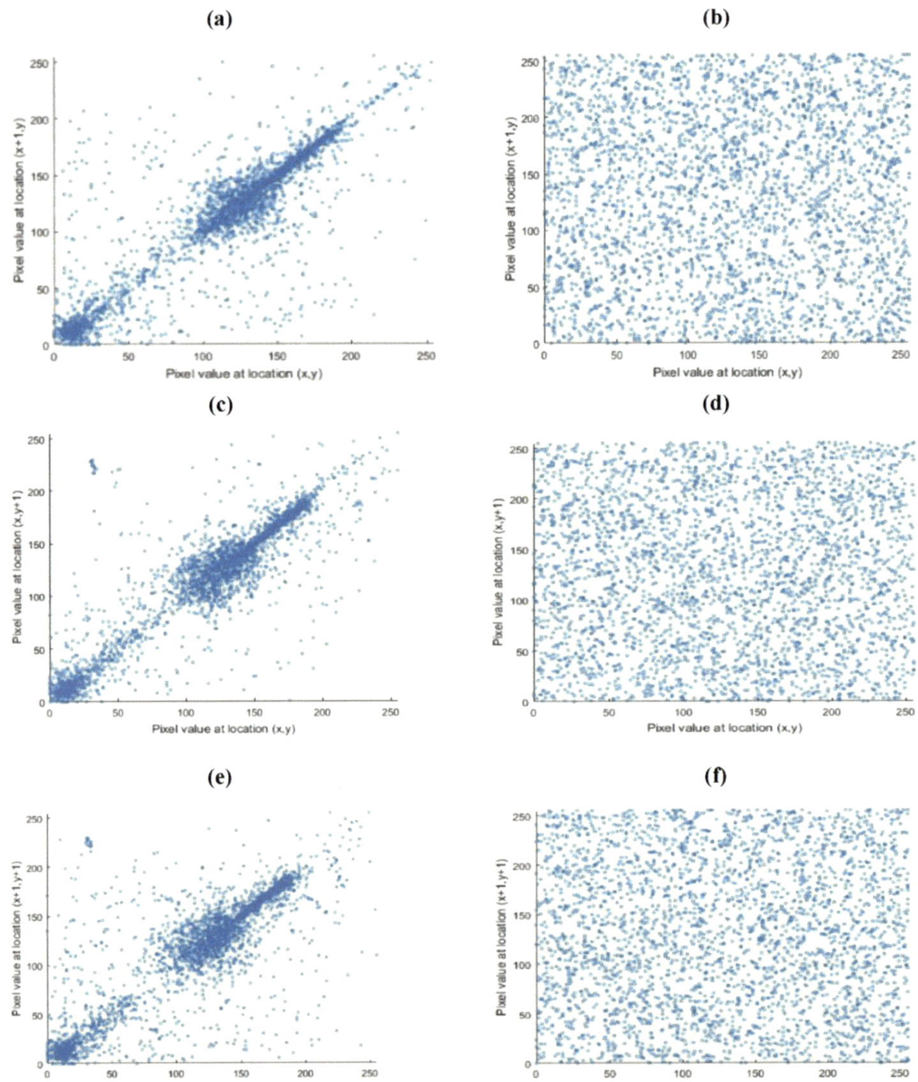

Figure 8.
Plot of correlation coefficients in horizontal, vertical, and diagonal directions of plain and cipher cameraman (512 × 512). (a, c, e) correlation coefficients of plain images in horizontal, vertical, and diagonal directions respectively. (b, d, f) correlation coefficients of ciphered images in horizontal, vertical, and diagonal directions respectively.

Imageq	Test	Plain image	Encrypted multiplex image 1 or 2
Cameraman	HC	0.9314	0.0023
	VC	0.9400	0.051
	DC	0.8931	−0.003
Peppers	HC	0.9934	0.0013
	VC	0.9954	−0.0020
	DC	0.9919	0.0044

Table 2.
Correlation coefficient.

images are not correlated in different directions. Then, these results prove that attacks based on correlation analysis cannot succeed on the proposed cryptosystem.

3.1.3 Information entropy analysis

The information entropy evaluates the level of randomness contained in a sequence m, and it is defined as follows:

$$S(m) = \sum_{i=0}^{2^M-1} p(m_i) \log_2\left(\frac{1}{p(m_i)}\right) \tag{20}$$

where $p(m_i)$ is the probability of the recurrence of element m_i and M denotes the number of bits of information m. The ideal entropy value of a 256-grayscale image represented on 8 bits with equal probability is 8. **Table 3** shows entropy values of the two multiplex images of the proposed encryption algorithm very close to 8, as expected.

3.2 Key analysis

Key space size is the total number of different keys that can be used in an encryption algorithm. A good encryption algorithm needs to contain sufficiently large key space to make the brute-force attack infeasible. The high sensitivity to initial conditions inherent to any chaotic system, that is, exponential divergence of chaotic trajectories, ensures high security [11].

In literature, a key space of at least 10^{30} is required for the system to be robust [19]. The proposed encryption algorithm actually does have some of the following secret keys: the initial values $x_{01}, x_{02}, x_{p1}, x_{p2}$ and control parameters $r_{01}, r_{02}, r_{p1}, r_{p2}$ and α of the chaotic systems used; the number N of target images and the size $M' \times M'$ of the filter. We suppose that the computer precision is 10^{-15}, so the key space is greater than $10^{15 \times 9} = 10^{135}$. Therefore, this key space is large enough to resist the brute-force attack. Moreover, key sensitivity analysis has been carried out, but the results are not presented here for reasons of space. These results confirm

Gray image	Proposed algorithm	[20] (2017)	[19] (2017)
Multiplex image 1	7.9993	—	—
Multiplex image 2	7.9993	7.9993	7.9992

Table 3.
Information entropy of some ciphered images.

Image	Test	
Multiplex encrypted image 1	NCPR	99.62
	UACI	33.54
Multiplex encrypted image 2	NCPR	99.63
	UACI	33.47

Table 4.
NCPR AND UACI measure after a LSB change.

that by changing only one bit in any parameter of the key, it is not possible to recover the plain images.

3.3 Sensitivity analysis

3.3.1 Differential attack analysis

An excellent encryption algorithm should have the desirable property of spreading the influence of slight change to the plain text over as much of the cipher text as possible. The sensitivity of a cryptosystem is evaluated through Number of Pixel Change Rate (NPCR), see Eq. (19), and Unified Average Change Intensity (UACI), see Eq. (20), criteria, which consist in testing the influence of one-pixel change of a plain image in the resulting cipher image.where C_1 and C_2 are two images with same size $W \times H$. If $C_1(\mathrm{i, j})$ # $C_2(\mathrm{i, j})$ $\mathrm{C_1(i,j) \neq C_2(i,j)}$ then $D(i,j) = 1$ $\mathrm{D(i,j) = 1}$, otherwise, $D(i,j) = 0$.

Table 4 gives the measurement of NCPR and UACI between two cipher images of cameraman, Lena and peppers, when a Least Significant Bit (LSB) changed on gray value in the last pixel's position. We can notice that the values obtained are around the mean of 99.61 for NCPR and 33.49 for UACI. This result shows that a slight change to the original images will result in a great change in all the encrypted images. The results also imply that the proposed algorithm has an excellent ability to resist the differential attack.

3.3.2 Quality of reconstructed images

As the number of target images to encrypt increases, the quality of recovered images decreases. In order to reduce the NMSE between plain and decrypted images and enlarge the number of target images, we grouped them into two multiplexed images before encryption. To evaluate quantitatively the quality of decrypted image, we used the normalized mean square error (NMSE) between the original image and the decrypted image. The NMSE is defined as:

$$\mathrm{NMSE} = \frac{\sum_{i=1}^{N}\sum_{j=1}^{M}[\mathrm{I_D(i,j)} - \mathrm{I_E(i,j)}]^2}{\sum_{i=1}^{N}\sum_{j=1}^{M}[\mathrm{I_E(i,j)}]^2} \tag{21}$$

where $\mathrm{M} \times \mathrm{N}$ are the size of the image, $\mathrm{I_D(i, j)}$ and $\mathrm{I_E(i, j)}$ are the values of the decrypted image and the original image at the pixel (i, j), respectively. **Table 5** presents the values of NMSE for a set of different target images of size 512×512. From this table, we can observe that for *N = 16* target images combined in one multiplex image, that is, 32 images to encrypt by the proposed cryptosystem, the NMSE is still low, which attests the good quality of reconstructed images and good performances of the proposed cryptosystem.

3.4 Encryption/decryption time

Table 6 reports a comparison of encryption time by the proposed algorithm with some recent works in literature for different images. The algorithm written under Matlab platform was not optimized. The computer time consumption is 0.27389 s, which is smaller than those of [19, 24].

3.5 Comparison with other encryption algorithms

The performance of the proposed algorithm compared to similar and good standing ones in literature is shown in **Table 7**. From the table, we can observe that the proposed encryption algorithm has a large key space and can encrypt a large number of target images in a good time compared to others. As for UACI and NPCR, they are about the best values expected (respectively >33.3 for UACI and >99.6 for NPCR) as can be seen in the table. Finally, our cryptosystem exhibits the best correlation value and a reduced normalized Mean Square Error (MSE) after decryption step.

Number of target images ($N \times 2$)	4×2	9×2	16×2
NMSE	0.00082	0.0019	0.00376

Table 5.
NMSE for a set of different target images.

Number of images	Proposed algorithm	[19] (2017)	[20] (2017)	[24] 2016
08 or 09, size 512×512	0.27389	0.7103	0.191	11.66

Table 6.
Encryption time in seconds.

	Key space	Average correlation	Entropy	NPCR	UACI	Encryption time (s)	NMSE
Proposed algorithm	10^{135}	0.0032	7.9993	99.61	33.49	0.27389	3.7×10^{-3}
Ref. [19] [2017]	10^{60}	0.003	7.9994	99.62	33.50	0.7103	—
Ref. [20] [2017]	10^{56}	—	7.8225	—	—	0.255	—
Ref. [24] [2016]	10^{90}	—	—	—	—	11.66	8.448×10^{-3}
Ref. [14] [2015]	2^{260}	0.0032	—	99.92	—	—	$\approx$**0**
Ref. [25] [2018]	10^{210}	0.0031	7.9986	99.62	33.42	2.386	0.0155

Table 7.
Comparison of the proposed cryptosystem with others.

4. Conclusion

In this chapter, an image encryption algorithm based on spectral fusion of multiple watermarked images and new chaotic generators is proposed. Logistic-May (LM), Gaussian-Gompertz (GG), and May-Gaussian (MG) systems were used as chaotic generators in the processes of confusion and diffusion. The target images were firstly combined in two multiplex images of same size through DCT and a low-pass filter. Secondly, the previous images are scrambled by permuting the blocks size of (4×4) of each multiplex image. Finally, the later scrambled images are fused by a nonlinear mathematical expression based on Cramer's rule to obtain two hybrid encrypted images. At the decryption step, the watermark hidden in one of the target images is recovered without loss of information. The evaluation metrics of the proposed cryptosystem NCPR, UACI, correlation coefficient, entropy, key space, and NMSE, are among the best values in literature. More interestingly, the proposed cryptosystem can encrypt 32 target images simultaneously with a small $\text{NMSE} \approx 4.16 \times 10^{-3} \approx 3.7 \times 10^{-3}$, and encrypted images are sensitive to the key. The proposed encryption algorithm can surely guarantee security and speed of all types of digital data (text and images) transfer in a digital network.

Acknowledgements

This work was partly supported by ERMIT, Entrepreneurship, Resources, Management, Innovation and Technologies.

Conflict of interest

The authors declare that they have no conflict of interest.

Author details

Lee Mariel Heucheun Yepdia[1], Alain Tiedeu[1*] and Zied Lachiri[2]

1 Signal, Image and Systems Laboratory, Department of Medical and Biomedical Engineering, Higher Technical Teachers Training College, University of Yaoundé, Ebolowa, Cameroon

2 Department of Electrical Engineering, Signal, Image and Technologies of Information Laboratory, National Engineering School, ENIT, Tunis, Tunisia

*Address all correspondence to: alain.tiedeu@gmail.com

References

[1] Liao X, Lai S, Zhou Q. A novel image encryption algorithm based on self-adaptive wave transmission. Journal of Signal Processing. 2010;**90**:2714-2722

[2] Zhu C. A novel image encryption scheme based on improved hyperchaotic sequences. Journal of Optical Communication. 2012;**285**:29-37

[3] Abanda Y, Tiedeu A. Image encryption by chaos mixing. IET Image Processing. 2016;**10**:742-750

[4] Wang X, Liu L, Zhang Y. A novel chaotic block image encryption algorithm based on dynamic random growth technique. Optics and Lasers in Engineering. 2015;**66**:10-18

[5] Rhouma R, Belghith S. Cryptanalysis of a spatiotemporal chaotic image/video cryptosystem. Physics Letters A. 2008; **A372**:5790-5794

[6] Wang Y, Liao X, Xiang T, Wong K, Yang D. Cryptanalysis and improvement on a block cryptosystem based on iteration a chaotic map. Physique Letters. 2007;**A363**:277-281

[7] Patidar V, Pareek N, Sud K. A new substitution-diffusion based image cipher using chaotic standard and logistic maps. Communications in Nonlinear Science and Numerical Simulation. 2009;**14**(7):3056-3075

[8] Zhu Z, Zhang W, Wong K, Yu H. A chaos-based symmetric image encryption scheme using a bit-level permutation. Information Sciences. 2011;**181**:1171-1186

[9] Song C, Qia Y, Zhang X. An image encryption scheme based on new spatiotemporal chaos. Optik. 2013;**124**: 3329-3334

[10] Gao H, Zhang Y, Liang S, Li D. A new chaotic algorithm for image encryption. Chaos, Solitons and Fractals. 2005;**29**:393-399

[11] Kamdeu Y, Tiedeu A. An image encryption algorithm based on substitution technique and chaos mixing. Multimedia Tools and Applications. 2018;**77**(19):1-22

[12] Chenaghlu M, Balafar M, Feizi-Derakhshi M. A novel image encryption algorithm based on polynomial combination of chaotic maps and dynamic function generation. Signal Processing. 2018;**157**:1-22

[13] Alfalou A, Brosseau C, Abdallah N. Simultaneous compression and encryption of color video images. Optics Communication. 2015;**338**:371-379

[14] Jridi M, Alfalou A. Real-time and encryption efficiency improvements of simultaneous fusion, compression and encryption method based on chaotic generators. Optics and Lasers in Engineering. 2018;**102**:59-69

[15] Alfalou A, Brosseau C, Abdallah N, Jridi M. Simultaneous fusion, compression and encryption of multiple images. Optics Express. 2011;**24**: 24023-24029

[16] Dongfeng S, Jian H, Yingjian W, Kee Y. Simultaneous fusion, imaging and encryption of multiple objects using a single-pixel detector. Scientific Reports. 2017;**7**:18-29

[17] Mehra I, Nishchal N. Wavelet-based image fusion for securing multiple images through asymmetric keys. Optics Communications. 2015;**335**:153-160

[18] Qin Y, Gong Q, Wang Z, Wang H. Optical multiple-image encryption in diffractive-imaging-based scheme using spectral fusion and nonlinear operation. Optics Express. 2016;**24**:26877-26886

[19] Zhang X, Wang X. Multiple-image encryption algorithm based on mixed image element and permutation. Optics and Lasers in Engineering. 2017;**92**:6-16

[20] Zhang X, Wang X. Multiple-image encryption algorithm based on mixed image element and chaos. Computers and Electrical Engineering. 2017;**000**: 1-13

[21] Zhu G, Zhang X. Mixed image element encryption based on an elliptic curve cryptosystem. Journal of Electronic Imaging. 2008;**17**(2):023007

[22] Abdalla A, Tamimi A. Algorithm for image mixing and encryption. The International Journal of Multimedia & Its Applications (IJMA). 2013;**5**(2):15-21

[23] Zhou Y, Bao L, Chen C. A new 1D chaotic system for image encryption. Signal Processing. 2014;**97**:172-182

[24] Ren G, Han J, Zhu H, Fu J, Shan M. High security multiple-image encryption using discrete cosine transform and discrete multiple-parameters fractional Fourier transform. The Journal of Communication. 2016;**11**(5):491-497

[25] Karawia A. Encryption algorithm of multiple-image using mixed image elements and two-dimensional chaotic economic map. Entropy. 2018;**20**:801. DOI: 10.3390/e20100801

[26] Al-Haj A, Mohammad A. Crypto-watermarking of transmitted medical images. Journal of Digital Imaging. 2017; **30**(1):26-38

[27] Abdel-Nabi H, Al-Haj A. Efficient joint encryption and data hiding algorithm for medical images security. In: 8th International Conference on Information and Communication Systems (ICICS). Irbid, Jordan: IEEE; 4-6 April 2017. pp. 147-152. DOI : 10.1109/IACS.2017.7921962

[28] Dagadu JC, Jianping L. Context-based watermarking cum chaotic encryption for medical images in telemedicine applications. Multimedia Tools and Applications. 2018;**77**: 24289-24312

[29] Maheshkar S. Region-based hybrid medical image watermarking for secure telemedicine applications. Multimedia Tools and Applications. 2017;**76**(3): 3617-3647

[30] Singh AK, Dave M, Mohan A. Robust and secure multiple watermarking in wavelet domain. Journal of Medical Imaging and Health Informatics. 2015;**5**(2):406-414

[31] Lian S, Liu Z, Yuan D, Wang H. On the joint audio fingerprinting and decryption scheme. In: IEEE International Conference on Multimedia and Expo; Hannover. 2008. pp. 261-264

[32] Abhilasha S, Kumar A, Singh S, Prakash G. Robust and secure multiple watermarking for medical images. Wireless Personal Communications. 2017;**92**:1611-1624

[33] Obin A, Varghese P. Image watermarking using DCT in selected pixel regions. In: International Conference on Control, Instrumentation, Communication and Computational Technologies (ICCICCT). Kanyakumari; 2014. pp. 398-402. DOI : 10.1109/ICCICCT.2014.6992994

Section 2

Bioinformation Analysis and Processing

Chapter 3

Information Extraction Techniques in Hyperspectral Imaging Biomedical Applications

Samuel Ortega, Martin Halicek, Himar Fabelo, Eduardo Quevedo, Baowei Fei and Gustavo Marrero Callico

Abstract

Hyperspectral imaging (HSI) is a technology able to measure information about the spectral reflectance or transmission of light from the surface. The spectral data, usually within the ultraviolet and infrared regions of the electromagnetic spectrum, provide information about the interaction between light and different materials within the image. This fact enables the identification of different materials based on such spectral information. In recent years, this technology is being actively explored for clinical applications. One of the most relevant challenges in medical HSI is the information extraction, where image processing methods are used to extract useful information for disease detection and diagnosis. In this chapter, we provide an overview of the information extraction techniques for HSI. First, we introduce the background of HSI, and the main motivations of its usage for medical applications. Second, we present information extraction techniques based on both light propagation models within tissue and machine learning approaches. Then, we survey the usage of such information extraction techniques in HSI biomedical research applications. Finally, we discuss the main advantages and disadvantages of the most commonly used image processing approaches and the current challenges in HSI information extraction techniques in clinical applications.

Keywords: hyperspectral imaging, biomedical, clinical, information extraction, machine learning, deep learning, image processing

1. Introduction

Hyperspectral imaging (HSI), also known as imaging spectroscopy, is a technology capable of sampling hundreds of narrow spectral bands across the electromagnetic spectrum through the use of an optical element that disperses the incoming radiation into certain wavelengths [1]. This technology combines the main features of two existing technologies: imaging and spectroscopy, making possible to exploit both the morphological features and the chemical composition of objects captured by a camera. The interaction between electromagnetic radiation and matter is distinctive for each material, therefore by using this technology it is possible to discriminate among different materials [2]. The characteristic spectral curve associated with a certain material is called spectral signature or spectral fingerprint, and through its analysis it

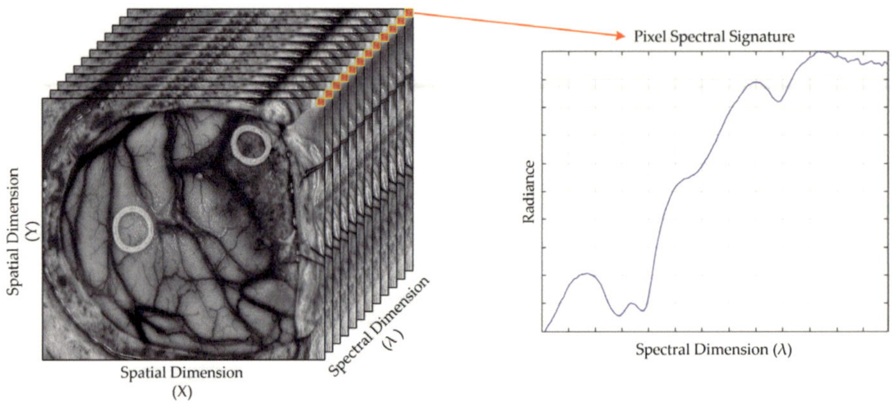

Figure 1.
Example of a HS cube with an example of a spectral signature.

is possible to differentiate among different materials or substances. The data structure used in HSI comprises both the spectral and spatial features from a given scene, and is referred to as hyperspectral (HS) cube. **Figure 1** shows a graphical representation of an HS cube with an example of a spectral signature for the top-right pixel.

Although historically HSI has been applied to remote sensing [3], in recent years this technology has become a trending topic in different research fields such as food quality analysis [4, 5], military and security applications [6] or agriculture [7, 8], among many others [9]. HSI is also an emerging imaging modality in the medical field. It has been proven that the interaction between the electromagnetic radiation and matter carries useful information for diagnostic proposes [10]. As an alternative diagnostic tool, one of the strengths offered by HSI is being completely non-invasive and label-free. In medical research applications, this technology has been employed for more than twenty years in different areas such as the analysis of cancerous tissues in *in-vivo* and *ex-vivo* samples [11], digital and computational pathology [12], melanoma detection [13] or several gastroenterology diseases [14].

In this chapter, a survey of the most common processing frameworks employed in the literature for information extraction in medical HSI will be presented. First, a brief introduction of the optical properties of biological tissues is provided. Second, the most common information extraction methods employed for HSI medical processing are described and discussed, including optical inverse modeling and machine learning methods. The last section summarizes the conclusions reached in this literature analysis.

2. Optical properties of biological tissue

The interaction between light and biological tissues has been proven to be a useful tool to identify and classify several diseases. Absorption, refraction and scattering are the three different types of interaction that can be measured in biological tissues [15]. Light absorption measures the amount of light absorbed and transformed to energy by tissue molecules. Specific wavelengths of the spectrum will present absorption peaks related to the transitions between two energy levels in a molecule, which can provide tissue diagnostic information. Absorption is the inverse measurement of reflectance using HSI systems. The measurement of refraction and reflection of light is based on changes in speed and direction of the incident light into tissue. Particularly, hemoglobin (Hb) is the major component of

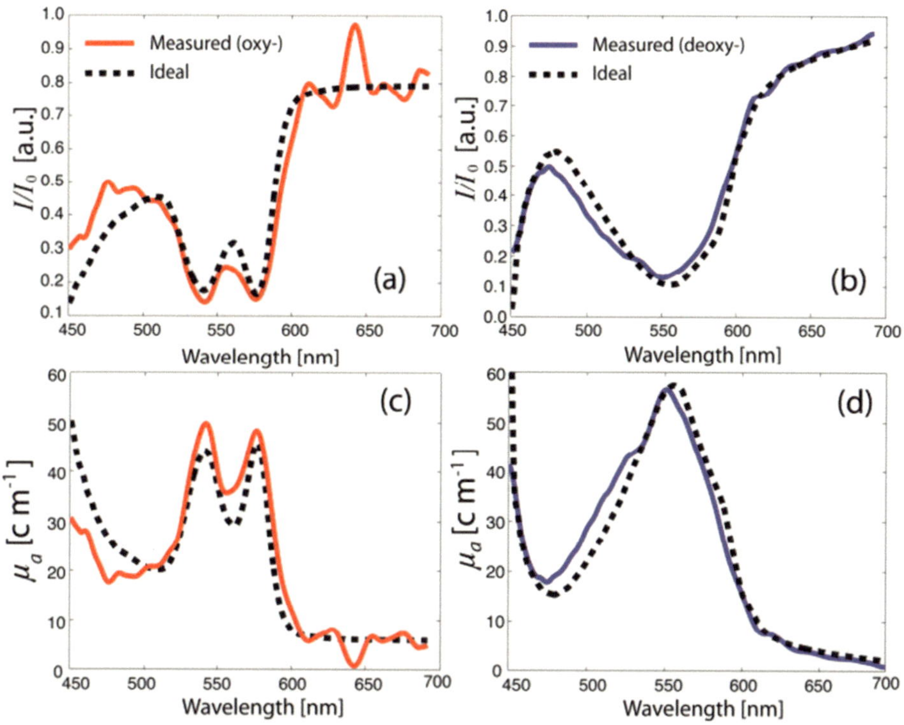

Figure 2.
Oxy-Hb (a) and deoxy-Hb (b) normalized absorption spectra, with Hb concentrations of 50 g/L and 68 g/L, respectively. The solid lines are experimentally measured, and the dotted black lines are the ideal. Oxy-Hb (c) and deoxy-Hb (d) measured and theoretical attenuation coefficients [18].

the spectral signature between 450 and 600 nm of biological tissues, and spectral differences can be observed in the absorption/reflectance between oxygenated and deoxygenated Hb states [16]. A single absorbance peak is found at 560 nm in deoxygenated Hb, while two absorbance peaks are found at 540 and 580 nm in oxygenated Hb [17]. **Figure 2** shows an example of these Hb signatures published in [18].

Regarding the measurement of light scattering, it is achieved when there is a spatial variation of the reflective index in the illuminated tissue. Scattering properties can be highly useful in diagnostic applications, since they provide different variations in tissue affected by a certain disease [19]. For example, the spectral range between 700 and 900 nm is related with the scattering dominant optical properties of collagen [20]. Also, the near-infrared spectral region is the scattering dominant region of fat, lipids, collagen, and water. Moreover, several tissues have fluorescence properties that can be revealed when such tissue is excited with certain wavelengths. As an example, ultraviolet light can be used to excite tissues, revealing the fluorescence emission of proteins and nucleic acids [21]. More details about biological tissue optical properties can be found in [19].

3. Information extraction methods for HSI

There are two main types of medical HSI processing: optical inverse modeling and machine learning approaches. In this section, both methods will be presented in detail, showing their main characteristics, as well as their advantages and disadvantages.

3.1 Optical inverse modeling

In optical inverse modeling techniques, a mathematical equation which models the interaction between the light and tissue is proposed, and the collected HS data is used to extract optical properties, such as the absorption or scattering of tissue. First, a physics-based model is proposed for the light propagation in tissues. Second, the HS data are used to extract optical properties from the proposed light propagation model. Although the number of studies which make use of this type of approach is limited, some researchers have used HS and light transport models in tissue to extract useful information for the detection of different diseases or conditions. Milanic *et al.* used Monte Carlo simulations of a light transport model in skin to extract information about the contents of melanin and blood saturation, with the goal of measuring cholesterol levels in human skin [22]. The same authors performed a similar processing analysis to skin HS data, but with the goal of detecting arthritis [23]. Claridge *et al.* demonstrated the utility of optical inverse modeling techniques for the estimation of the blood volume fraction of ex-vivo colon samples, showing statistically significant differences between the blood volume fraction of tumor and healthy conditions [24].

The use of optical inverse modeling for information extraction in medical HSI presents some advantages and challenges. The main advantage is to count with an established physical-based model for correlating measured data, which are theoretically strong and contain tissue optical parameters that can be used for diagnostics. The main disadvantage of this approach is the possibility of bias in the model development and over-simplification of complex physical processes, which could result in suboptimal performance for information extraction.

3.2 Machine learning methods

Machine Learning (ML) methods are algorithms able to learn from data. ML algorithms enable solutions to difficult tasks which usually cannot be performed by a traditionally designed computer program [25]. There are different ML algorithms depending on the task they perform. In regression problems, a numerical variable is estimated from the data. In the context of medical HSI, Arimoto *et al.* used regression techniques to estimate the oxygen saturation map from human retina [26]. In classification problems, the objective is to assign a data sample to a fixed category. For example, Fabelo *et al.* used classification to identify normal tissue, tumor tissue, hypervascularized tissue and background in HS images from in-vivo human brain tissue [27]. The results of the classification of a medical HS image are usually represented as a classification map or heat map, where different colors are used for each class (**Figure 3**).

ML algorithms can be classified as supervised and unsupervised. In unsupervised algorithms, the goal is to cluster similar data samples in groups, extracting the information from data features. In supervised algorithms, the data is comprised of the data features and associated labels [29]. For example, in the example of **Figure 3A**, the data features consist of the spectra of each pixel of the HS image, and the labels are the different categories into which each pixel can be categorized, i.e. normal tissue, tumor tissue, hypervascularized tissue and background. The main goal of supervised algorithms is to use data and their labels to train a model which can be used to perform predictions about new data. ML techniques can be categorized as Feature Learning (FL) or Deep Learning (DL) methods. In FL approaches, the inputs of a supervised classifier are given by features extracted from the data. For example, in an image processing framework, such features may be related to shape, texture or color. On the contrary, DL approaches are devoted

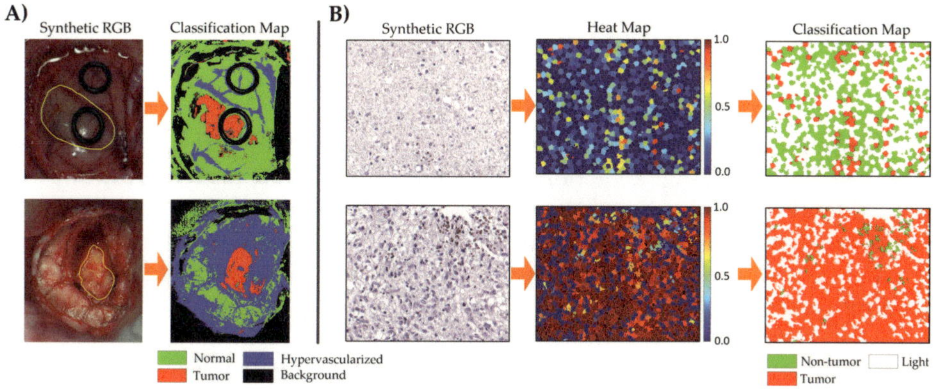

Figure 3.
Example of classification and heat maps obtained through ML classification from (A) in-vivo brain tissue HS images [27] and (B) in-vitro H&E brain tissue HS images [28].

to use all the data as input to a supervised classifier, and the important features to perform the classification task are learned by the supervised classifier.

There are challenges related with both types of ML approaches. On the one hand, in FL methods, the classification may be biased by which features are selected from the data for the classification, while the identification of features is performed automatically in a DL algorithm. On the other hand, DL methods usually require large amounts of data to succeed in the feature extraction and classification, while FL approaches may provide good performance with a limited dataset. Next, we provide a survey about the different ML approaches which are commonly used for HSI processing in medical applications.

3.2.1 Feature learning

In this section, we describe the most common FL approaches which have been employed for processing medical HS data. This section is categorized in three main categories, namely pixel-wise classification, feature extraction and selection methods, and the usage of both the spatial and spectral information.

3.2.1.1 Pixel-wise classifiers

In the HS literature, the concept of pixel-wise processing refers to the exclusive usage of the spectral information within an HS cube for extracting information from HS data. Recently, Ghamisi *et al.* performed a survey between the most commonly used classifiers in pixel-wise classification of HS images [30]. The most common classifiers used for the classification of HS images from a feature learning perspective are Support Vector Machines (SVMs), Random Forest (RF) and Multinomial Logistic Regression (MLR) based approaches.

SVM is a binary classification algorithm proposed by Vapnik [31]. The algorithm finds the optimal hyperplane that maximizes the margin between samples belonging to different classes. Although it was originally designed for linear classification, an SVM classifier can be used for nonlinear classification problems by using different kernels to map the data into a higher dimensional space. SVM has been shown to provide competitive classification performance on HS data even with a limited training sample size [32].

RF was firstly proposed by Breiman [33]. This algorithm consists of an ensemble of decision trees, where, in each decision tree, the training data are hierarchically partitioned into smaller homogeneous groups. In RF, different decision trees are generated from the training data, and the different classification results are combined by a voting process. The main advantage of RF is a reduced training time. RF has been successfully used for the classification of HS images [34].

Finally, MLR [35] approaches exploit the posterior class distributions of the training data for making predictions, and these methods have been successfully applied for the classification of HS images. The main advantages of MLR are fast computation for training and customizability, which allows modifications to the original algorithm to provide better generalization, e.g. sparsity constraints or multiple feature learning.

In the context of medical HS classification, several authors have utilized the spectral information for the diagnosis of different diseases in a pixel-wise manner. The most commonly used pixel-wise classifier in medical HSI is SVM. In the context of surgical guidance, Akbari *et al.* processed HS images from the abdomen to detect intestinal ischemia [36]. For cancer detection, SVM and HSI have been used for the identification of gastric cancer [37], prostate cancer [38], tongue cancer [39], and skin cancer [40]. Although RF and MLR have been widely used for HS information extraction, their usage in medical HSI is limited. RF has been used for the detection of in-vivo oral cancer [41], while MLR has been considered for identification of ulcerative colitis in histological slides [42]. The main challenge in this field is to determine which pixel-wise classifier is more suitable for the classification of certain HS data. In this sense, some authors have performed comparisons of performance of different pixel-wise classifiers for the detection of brain cancer in histological slides [43], or the detection of the tumor margins in head and neck ex-vivo tissue [44]. Although SVM has been shown to outperform other classifiers, a deeper comparison between different classifiers should be urgently performed to definitively demonstrate which pixel-wise classifier performs better with HSI across multiple applications.

3.2.1.2 Feature extraction and feature selection

HS data are characterized by a high dimensionality. For this reason, instead of exploiting the complete spectral signature for image analysis, one trend in HSI processing is the use of Dimensionality Reduction (DR) methods. These methods are devoted to reduce dimensionality of the original data while preserving the most relevant information [45]. DR methods have been extensively used for HS image processing. There are two main types of DR approaches: feature extraction and feature selection methods.

On the one hand, in feature extraction methods, a transformation is applied to the data to generate a new representation with lower dimensionality, but similar information content. The most studied DR algorithm for HSI is Principal Component Analysis (PCA). The goal of PCA [46] is searching for a linear transformation of the data by using orthogonal projections which minimize the covariance matrix of the original data. On the other hand, several data transformation approaches have been proposed for dimensionality reduction, such as wavelet transformations [47], different orthogonal projection approaches, or the exploitation of manifold embedding [48].

Nevertheless, in feature extraction methods the data are transformed, and thus the physical information about specific wavelengths is lost, which means that the provided interaction between light and tissue cannot be analyzed, which may affect certain applications. For this reason, feature selection methods are devoted to find the most relevant features from the original data by keeping the most relevant information. In the context of HSI, feature selection methods are also known as band selection methods, which also seek to identify the most relevant spectral features for a certain application. There are several types of band selection methods. In this chapter, we only describe the most prominent methods used in medical HSI. In a large-dissimilarity criteria approach, the goal is to select the most dissimilar spectral bands. Conversely, in a low-correlation criterion, the spectral bands showing low correlation between each other are selected. An example of this kind of algorithm is Maximum Relevance Minimum Redundancy (mRMR). In search-based methods, the band selection is performed by solving an optimization problem driven by a given optimization function. These algorithms search for the best bands to solve such optimization problem. Some search-based methods used in HSI are Genetic Algorithm (GA) [49] or Particle Swarm Optimization (PSO) [50]. Further details about more sophisticated band selection techniques can be found in [51].

In the context of medical HSI, feature extraction methods are used both as standalone methods and as a preprocessing stage before further data analysis. The former approach is to enhance the visualization of data, while the latter reduces the complexity of the data for being processed by other machine learning approaches. As an example of the direct application of PCA for tissue visualization enhancement, Zuzak *et al.* applied PCA to abdominal HS images in order to enhance the visualization of biliary trees using in-vivo samples [52]. Also, Wilson *et al.* demonstrated the ability of HSI for melanin detection in histological unstained specimens of melanocytic lesions in the skin and the eye using PCA and false-color representations of data [53]. PCA has been used for extracting the most important features of HS data prior to classification in different applications, such as the detection of in-vivo oral cancer [54], prostate cancer in histological slides [55], the identification of white blood cells in blood smear slides [56] or the intraoperative delineation of brain tumors [57]. Another example of the utility of feature extraction methods was demonstrated by Hadoux *et al.*, where relevant differences between the retinal spectral data from patients with Alzheimer and healthy patients were found after applying an orthogonal projection of data [58]. Such differences in the spectral signature from different disease states were not possible using the raw spectral signature of tissue. Beyond PCA and orthogonal projection methods, Ravi *et al.* proposed a modification of the t-Distributed Stochastic Neighbor Embedding feature extraction algorithm, a non-linear dimensionality reduction technique, prior to the identification of tumor tissue within in-vivo brain samples [59]. Other feature extraction methods used in medical HSI prior to classification are the use of wavelet transformation for the detection of prostate cancer in mice models [60], or the use of Fourier Series coefficients for breast cancer detection [61].

The use of band selection methods for medical HSI applications is not as extended as in other fields, such as remote sensing. However, some researchers have successfully exploited different band selection methods in HSI. Goto *et al.* used the Mahalanobis distance to determine the optimal wavelengths for gastric cancer, correctly identifying normal and tumor mucosa [62]. Additionally, mRMR has been used for the identification of the most relevant bands for ex-vivo breast cancer detection [61], and for in-vivo head and neck cancer [63]. Finally, Martinez-Vega *et al.* proposed a search-based method based on different optimization algorithms for the identification of the most relevant wavelengths for brain tumor detection within in-vivo HS images [64]. The optimization function was the pixel-wise classification performance metrics obtained by an SVM classifier. The results demonstrated that a GA optimization slightly improves tumor identification compared to the full-spectra counterpart.

Both feature selection and feature extraction methods aim to reduce the dimensionality of HS data while retaining the most important information. Successful application of these techniques leads to reduced computational time, which is required in applications such as surgical guidance. Nevertheless, for biomedical HS applications, there are some relevant advantages of using band selection methods instead of feature extraction methods. The first advantage is that the information about the concrete wavelengths that are used is retained. This fact allows further analysis about the physical response of different tissues to specific wavelengths. The second advantage of band selection methods is the possibility of developing custom HS cameras which only captures the most relevant spectral channels for a given application. Such reduced-band cameras would be able to acquire HS video, which would be also convenient for some surgical guidance applications.

3.2.1.3 Spatial-spectral information

Although the aforementioned data processing methods rely on the spectral information, a HS cube is a 3D data structure containing both the spatial and the spectral information of a scene. In a recent review manuscript, He *et al.* provided a survey about different spatial-spectral techniques which have been used for the classification of HSI [65]. The inclusion of both spectral and spatial information is motivated by the limitations found in the spectral data. First, the high dimensionality of spectral data together with a limited dataset can lead to the *curse of dimensionality*. This phenomenon offers more detailed information about the captured scene, but it also contains redundant information and increases the computational time required to process the data [4]. Second, the high variability shown in the spectral data due to different lighting conditions, instrumentation noise, or other phenomena, makes the classification based only on the spectral information a challenge. In addition, high intra-class and low inter-class variability of the spectral signatures produces difficulties in the differentiation between classes. This problem is particularly challenging in biomedical data, where data originate from multiple patients. For these reasons, researchers within the HSI processing community have successfully improved the classification of pixel-wise approaches by the utilization of spatial and spectral features from HS images.

In [65], the authors proposed a classification of spatial-spectral approaches in three main types, depending on how the spatial information is integrated in the processing framework. In pre-processing approaches, spatial and spectral features are extracted from the HS cube, and then such features are used for the classification. In integrated classification, both spatial and spectral features are used to train the classifier. Finally, in post-processing approaches, the spatial information is employed to refine the results of a pixel-wise processing of the HS cube.

In the context of medical HSI processing, most of the spatial-spectral approaches have been focused in pre-processing and post-processing schemes. Some pre-processing approaches are the following. In leukemia detection in blood smear slides, Wang *et al.* evaluated the usage of three types of inputs for a supervised classifier: spatial features, spectral features, and spatial-spectral features. The results of this study suggest that the exploitation of both the spatial and the spectral features significantly improves the quality of the classification [66]. Similarly, Li *et al.* evaluated the feasibility of utilizing HSI for Red Blood Cell (RBC) counting. After conducting the RBC counting using uniquely spatial or spectral features of blood cells, the authors found an improvement in the under-counting and over-counting rates when they performed the image analysis using both types of features together [67]. Ortega *et al.* make use of the spatial information of the HS data by performing superpixel segmentation [68]. In post-processing approaches, Fabelo *et al.* proposed the incorporation of the spatial information to the SVM pixel-wise classification by using a K-nearest neighbors spatial filter which makes use of a one-dimensional representation of the HS cube extracted using PCA for the identification of in-vivo brain tumor [57].

3.2.2 Deep learning methods

Deep Learning is a family of machine learning algorithms that learn abstract features to best represent and make predictions about new data that is presented. More specifically, neural networks (NNs) consist of consecutive layers of neurons that have non-linear activations that connect the input data, extract features, and connect to logical outputs representing the classes of labels to provide prediction probabilities. Neural networks can have various dimensionalities, which largely depends on the size and dimensions of the input data. For example, utilizing only spectral signature information, a 1-D NN can extract features with fully-connected layers or 1-D convolutions. However, HS cameras acquire spatial information and spectral signatures simultaneously. Therefore, to exploit both sets of features, pseudo 3-D HS data can be input directly into a 2D-CNN and extract spatial features with learned convolutional kernels in the spatial domain, and these filters are connected across the entire spectral domain of the HS data. Lastly, 3D-CNN can utilize the full pseudo 3D HS data as input and extract spatial-spectral features with 3D convolutional kernels. There are numerous approaches, but these methods require more computational processing as more features and dimensions are involved.

The most widely used approach is 2D-CNNs. Aggressive brain tumors, such as glioblastoma, often require surgical resection for treatment, and surgeons often implement multiple imaging modalities, including fluorescence, to aid in this very challenging task. In a pilot study to aid brain surgeons with label-free HSI, Fabelo *et al.* compared both 2D-CNN and 1D-DNN, considering spectral-only and spectral-spatial classification using DL [69]. In HSI digital histology, Ortega *et al.* detected glioblastoma brain cancer in digital slides using a patch-based 2D-CNN approach [70]. Additionally, Halicek *et al.* has employed very deep 2D-CNNs for classification, specifically the widely-used Inception v4 model (**Figure 4**) implemented in a sliding patch-based approach for head and neck squamous cancer [71] and thyroid and salivary gland cancers [72]. For comparing 2D-CNN and 3D-CNNs, in [73] Halicek *et al.* explored spatial-spectral convolutions in 3D CNNs with 3D convolutional kernels to 2D approaches. Although data were limited to only 12 patients, the preliminary results suggest 3D convolutions outperformed 2D convolutions for CNN design at the cost of computational power and speed.

Another desired application of DL for HSI is semantic segmentation, which allows the entire scene to be classified altogether from spectral-spatial features in the entire scene. Semantic segmentation does not require image reconstruction like patch-based 2D-CNN approaches. The most commonly used method is the U-Net, as first used in

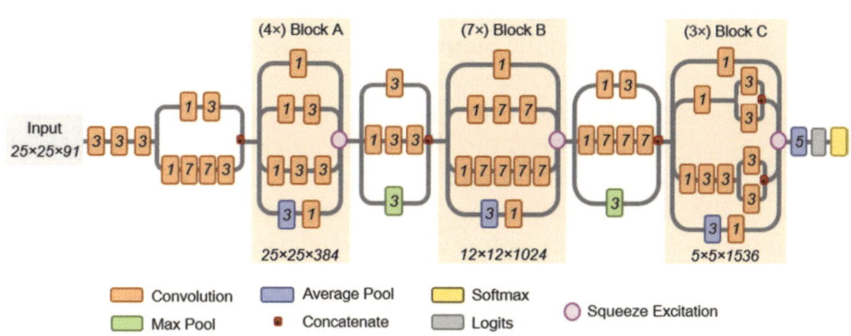

Figure 4.
Schematic diagram of the modified inception v4 CNN architecture. The CNN was customized to operate on the 25 × 25 × 91 patch-size selected. The receptive field size and number of convolutional filters is shown at bottom of each inception block. The convolutional kernel size used for convolutions is shown in italics inside each convolution box. Squeeze-and-excitation modules were added to the CNN to increase performance [72].

HSI by Trajanovski *et al.* for tongue cancer detection with a 2D input data using all HS channels for semantic segmentation of ex-vivo specimens [74]. Additionally, Kho et al. used ex-vivo specimens from patients with breast cancer and applied a standard U-net with 2D input HS data using all spectral channels for semantic segmentation [75].

More recently, several modern DL approaches with origins in computer-vision have been applied to medical HSI experimentally. In [76], a generative adversarial network (GAN) was applied to use DL to learn the association of RGB images and HS images to learn the ability to generate HS digital histology images from standard RGB digital histology images of breast cancer. Another modern approach is long-short-term-memory (LSTM) and recurrent neural networks (RNN) which can utilize spatial-spectral and time-based inputs to operate in real-time video approaches. In [77], RNNs are compared to and outperform 2D- and 3D-CNN methods for in-vivo cancer detection with the goal of real-time video endoscopy.

The use of DL for HS processing is currently a hot topic in the research community in different fields. The main advantage of DL approaches in HSI is their capability to exploit jointly the spatial and the spectral information for image processing tasks. Currently, researchers are experimenting with different DL architectures in order to find the most appropriate DL model for HSI [78]. In the context of medical HSI, the use of DL in medical HS have shown good performance in different applications, but its usage is still limited compared to other ML approaches. The main reason is the limited number of data due to the novelty of the technology. More publicly available datasets with a large number of patients are required in order to definitively establish an adequate comparative of DL and traditional ML techniques.

4. Conclusions

In this book chapter, we provide a survey about the most common processing frameworks for information extraction in medical HSI. First, we show the main motivations on the usage of HS technology for biomedical data: the interaction between the light and tissue provides useful information for diagnostic applications. Second, we survey the most common approaches for HSI processing in the medical field: inverse optical modeling and machine learning approaches.

Within the ML approaches, we show there is a big variety in the methods which are used, mainly in two different types: traditional machine learning approaches based handcrafted features and recent DL techniques. Even within each subfield, the variety of options to extract information in medical HSI is still wide.

In **Table 1** we provide a summary of the applications of the different methods which have been described in this book chapter. Such table relates the main information extraction methods and the biomedical applications of HSI. Further literature revision about the different biomedical HSI applications are out of the scope of this chapter. However, we recommend readers who are interested in further information about the usage of HSI for different biomedical applications to refer the different literature reviews in this context mentioned in the introduction section.

The main challenge in HS medical image processing is to determine which processing framework is the most appropriate for clinical applications. Nowadays, the current trend for researchers working with medical HS data is to collect their own data, and then propose a processing framework to address a certain problem. Normally such processing frameworks are customized for their particular applications. In order to reach an agreement by the research community on the most successful information extraction methods for HSI, there is the need of further investigations with comparisons among the most promising processing approaches. To this end, the availability of large public datasets would help. However, although there is no general

Information extraction method		**Algorithm**	**Application**	**Ref.**
Optical inverse modeling		Light transport models and Monte Carlo Simulations	Cholesterol identification in skin	[22]
			Arthritis identification in skin	[23]
			Blood volume fraction estimation in colon cancer samples	[24]
Feature learning	Pixel-wise classification	SVM	Intestinal ischemia identification	[36]
			Gastric cancer detection	[37]
			Prostate cancer	[38]
			Tongue cancer	[39]
			Skin cancer	[40]
		RF	In-vivo oral cancer	[41]
		MLR	Ulcerative colitis in histological slides	[42]
		SVM, RF	Brain cancer in histological slides	[43]
		SVM, RF, LDA	Head and neck tumor	[44]
	Feature extraction and feature selection	PCA	Biliary trees visualization enhancement	[52]
		PCA and false color	Melanocytic lesions visualization	[53]
		PCA and supervised classification	Detection of in-vivo oral cancer	[54]
			Prostate cancer in histological slides	[55]
			The identification of white blood cells in blood smear slides	[56]
			Intraoperative brain tumor delineation	[57]
		Orthogonal projections	Retina analysis for Alzheimer's detection	[58]
		t-SNE and supervised classification	In-vivo brain tumor detection	[59]
		Wavelet transformation and supervised classification	Prostate cancer in mice models	[60]
		Fourier series and supervised classification	Breast cancer detection	[61]
		Band selection with Mahalanobis distance	Gastric cancer identification	[62]
		Band selection with mRMR	Ex-vivo breast cancer detection	[61]
			In-vivo head and neck cancer	[63]
		Band selection with optimization techniques	In-vivo brain tumor detection ‡	[64]
	Spatial-spectral classification	Spatial and spectral features in supervised classification	Leukemia detection in blood smear	[66]
			Red blood cell counting	[67]
		Superpixel segmentation and supervised classification	Brain tumor detection in histological slides	[68]
		Supervised classification and K-NN spatial filtering	In-vivo brain tumor detection‡	[27]
Deep learning		2D-CNN and 1D-DNN	In-vivo brain tumor detection‡	[69]
		2D-CNN (Inception v4)	Head and neck cancer	[71]
			Salivary gland cancer	[72]
		2D-CNN and 3D-CNN	Head and neck cancer	[73]
		2D-CNN (U-Net)	Tongue cancer detection	[74]
			Breast cancer	[75]
		GAN	HS image generation from RGB	[76]
		RNNs, 2D-CNN and 3D-CNN	Head and neck cancer detection	[77]

Publicly available datasets are marked with ‡.

Table 1.
Summary of information extraction methods for medical HSI.

processing framework, the different information extraction techniques together with HS medical data have demonstrated several advantages for biomedical applications.

Acknowledgements

This research was supported in part by the Canary Islands Government through the ACIISI (Canarian Agency for Research, Innovation and the Information Society), ITHACA project under Grant Agreement ProID2017010164 and by the Spanish Government through PLATINO project (TEC2017-86722-C4-4-R). This research was supported in part by the Cancer Prevention and Research Institute of Texas (CPRIT) grant RP190588 and the U.S. National Institutes of Health (NIH) grants (R01CA156775, R01CA204254, R01HL140325, and R21CA231911). This work was completed while Samuel Ortega was beneficiary of a pre-doctoral grant given by the "*Agencia Canaria de Investigacion, Innovacion y Sociedad de la Información (ACIISI)*" of the "*Conserjería de Economía, Industria, Comercio y Conocimiento*" of the "*Gobierno de Canarias,*" which is part-financed by the European Social Fund (FSE) (*POC 2014-2020, Eje 3 Tema Prioritario 74 (85%)*).

Conflict of interest

The authors declare that there are no conflicts of interest related to this chapter.

Author details

Samuel Ortega[1*], Martin Halicek[2,3], Himar Fabelo[1], Eduardo Quevedo[1], Baowei Fei[4,5,6] and Gustavo Marrero Callico[1]

1 Research Institute for Applied Microelectronics, University of Las Palmas de Gran Canaria, Las Palmas de Gran Canaria, Spain

2 Department of Biomedical Engineering, Emory University and Georgia Institute of Technology, Atlanta, GA, USA

3 Medical College of Georgia, Augusta University, Augusta, GA, USA

4 Department of Bioengineering, University of Texas at Dallas, Dallas, TX, USA

5 Advanced Imaging Research Center, University of Texas Southwestern Medical Center, Dallas, TX, USA

6 Department of Radiology, University of Texas Southwestern Medical Center, Dallas, TX, USA

*Address all correspondence to: sortega@iuma.ulpgc.es

References

[1] Kamruzzaman M, Sun D-W. Introduction to Hyperspectral Imaging Technology. In: Computer Vision Technology for Food Quality Evaluation [Internet]. Elsevier; 2016 [cited 2018 Sep 11]. p. 111-39. Available from: https://www.sciencedirect.com/science/article/pii/B9780128022320000050

[2] Soares JANT. Introduction to Optical Characterization of Materials. In: Practical Materials Characterization. Springer Nature; 2014. p. 43-92.

[3] Sudharsan S, Hemalatha R, Radha S. A survey on hyperspectral imaging for mineral exploration using machine learning algorithms. In: 2019 International Conference on Wireless Communications, Signal Processing and Networking, WiSPNET 2019. Institute of Electrical and Electronics Engineers Inc.; 2019. p. 206-12.

[4] Lei T, Sun DW. Developments of nondestructive techniques for evaluating quality attributes of cheeses: A review. Vol. 88, Trends in Food Science and Technology. Elsevier Ltd; 2019. p. 527-42.

[5] Vejarano R, Siche R, Tesfaye W. Evaluation of biological contaminants in foods by hyperspectral imaging: A review. Int J Food Prop [Internet]. 2017 Jun 8 [cited 2020 Apr 22];20: 1-34. Available from: https://www.tandfonline.com/doi/full/10.1080/10942912.2017.1338729

[6] Shimoni M, Haelterman R, Perneel C. Hypersectral imaging for military and security applications: Combining Myriad processing and sensing techniques. IEEE Geosci Remote Sens Mag. 2019 Jun 1;7(2):101-17.

[7] Mishra P, Asaari MSM, Herrero-Langreo A, Lohumi S, Diezma B, Scheunders P. Close range hyperspectral imaging of plants: A review. Vol. 164, Biosystems Engineering. Academic Press; 2017. p. 49-67.

[8] Adão T, Hruška J, Pádua L, Bessa J, Peres E, Morais R, et al. Hyperspectral imaging: A review on UAV-based sensors, data processing and applications for agriculture and forestry. Remote Sens. 2017;9(11).

[9] Khan MJ, Khan HS, Yousaf A, Khurshid K, Abbas A. Modern Trends in Hyperspectral Image Analysis: A Review. Vol. 6, IEEE Access. Institute of Electrical and Electronics Engineers Inc.; 2018. p. 14118-29.

[10] Lu G, Fei B. Medical hyperspectral imaging: a review. J Biomed Opt [Internet]. 2014;19(1):10901. Available from: http://www.pubmedcentral.nih.gov/articlerender.fcgi?artid=3895860&tool=pmcentrez&rendertype=abstract

[11] Halicek M, Fabelo H, Ortega S, Callico GM, Fei B. In-Vivo and Ex-Vivo Tissue Analysis through Hyperspectral Imaging Techniques: Revealing the Invisible Features of Cancer. Cancers (Basel) [Internet]. 2019 May 30;11(6):756. Available from: https://www.mdpi.com/2072-6694/11/6/756

[12] Ortega S, Halicek M, Fabelo H, Callico GM, Fei B. Hyperspectral and multispectral imaging in digital and computational pathology: a systematic review [Invited]. Biomed Opt Express [Internet]. 2020 Jun 1 [cited 2020 May 22];11(6):3195. Available from: https://www.osapublishing.org/abstract.cfm?URI=boe-11-6-3195

[13] Johansen TH, Møllersen K, Ortega S, Fabelo H, Garcia A, Callico GM, et al. Recent advances in hyperspectral imaging for melanoma detection. Wiley Interdiscip Rev Comput Stat [Internet]. 2019 Apr 22 [cited 2019 May 17];e1465.

Available from: https://onlinelibrary.wiley.com/doi/abs/10.1002/wics.1465

[14] Ortega S, Fabelo H, Iakovidis D, Koulaouzidis A, Callico G, Ortega S, et al. Use of Hyperspectral/Multispectral Imaging in Gastroenterology. Shedding Some–Different–Light into the Dark. J Clin Med [Internet]. 2019 Jan 1 [cited 2019 Jan 12];8(1):36. Available from: http://www.mdpi.com/2077-0383/8/1/36

[15] Tuchin V V. Tissue optics: Light scattering methods and instruments for medical diagnosis: Third edition [Internet]. Tuchin V, editor. Tissue Optics: Light Scattering Methods and Instruments for Medical Diagnosis: Third Edition. SPIE; 2015 [cited 2020 Mar 27]. 1-935 p. Available from: file:///C:/Users/Cooper/Downloads/PM254_ch2.pdf

[16] Chen P-C, Lin W-C. Spectral-profile-based algorithm for hemoglobin oxygen saturation determination from diffuse reflectance spectra. Biomed Opt Express [Internet]. 2011 May 1 [cited 2019 Mar 20];2(5):1082. Available from: https://www.osapublishing.org/boe/abstract.cfm?uri=boe-2-5-1082

[17] Eaton WA, Hanson LK, Stephens PJ, Sutherland JC, Dunn JBR. Optical spectra of oxy- and deoxyhemoglobin. J Am Chem Soc [Internet]. 1978 Aug [cited 2019 Mar 20];100(16):4991-5003. Available from: http://pubs.acs.org/doi/abs/10.1021/ja00484a013

[18] Robles FE, Chowdhury S, Wax A. Assessing hemoglobin concentration using spectroscopic optical coherence tomography for feasibility of tissue diagnostics. Biomed Opt Express [Internet]. 2010 Jul 27 [cited 2018 Dec 31];1(1):310-7. Available from: http://www.ncbi.nlm.nih.gov/pubmed/21258468

[19] Jacques SL. Optical properties of biological tissues: a review. Phys Med Biol [Internet]. 2013 May 7 [cited 2019 Mar 20];58(11):R37-61. Available from: http://stacks.iop.org/0031-9155/58/i=11/a=R37?key=crossref.e58b67eb50f9f6507dd5e75b7744fa07

[20] Sekar SKV, Bargigia I, Mora AD, Taroni P, Ruggeri A, Tosi A, et al. Diffuse optical characterization of collagen absorption from 500 to 1700 nm. J Biomed Opt [Internet]. 2017 Jan 31 [cited 2019 Mar 20];22(1):015006. Available from: http://www.ncbi.nlm.nih.gov/pubmed/28138693

[21] Excited States of Proteins and Nucleic Acids. Excited States of Proteins and Nucleic Acids. Springer US; 1971.

[22] Milanic M, Bjorgan A, Larsson M, Strömberg T, Randeberg LL. Detection of hypercholesterolemia using hyperspectral imaging of human skin. In: Brown JQ, Deckert V, editors. ProcSPIE - European Conference on Biomedical Optics [Internet]. SPIE-Intl Soc Optical Eng; 2015. p. 95370C. Available from: http://proceedings.spiedigitallibrary.org/proceeding.aspx?doi=10.1117/12.2183880

[23] Milanic M, Paluchowski LA, Randeberg LL. Hyperspectral imaging for detection of arthritis: feasibility and prospects. J Biomed Opt [Internet]. 2015 Sep;20(9):096011. Available from: http://biomedicaloptics.spiedigitallibrary.org/article.aspx?doi=10.1117/1.JBO.20.9.096011

[24] Claridge E, Hidović-Rowe D, Taniere P, Ismail T. Quantifying mucosal blood volume fraction from multispectral images of the colon. In: Manduca A, Hu XP, editors. Medical Imaging 2007: Physiology, Function, and Structure from Medical Images. SPIE; 2007.

[25] Goodfellow I, Bengio Y, Courville A. Deep Learning. The MIT Press; 2016.

[26] Arimoto H, Furukawa H. Retinal blood oxygen saturation mapping

by multispectral imaging and morphological angiography. In: Annual International Conference of the IEEE Engineering in Medicine and Biology - Proceedings. 2007. p. 1627-30.

[27] Fabelo H, Ortega S, Ravi D, Kiran BR, Sosa C, Bulters D, et al. Spatio-spectral classification of hyperspectral images for brain cancer detection during surgical operations. Fred AL, editor. PLoS One [Internet]. 2018 Mar 19;13(3):e0193721. Available from: https://doi.org/10.1371/journal.pone.0193721

[28] Ortega S, Fabelo H, Halicek M, Camacho R, Plaza M de la L, Callicó GM, et al. Hyperspectral Superpixel-Wise Glioblastoma Tumor Detection in Histological Samples. Appl Sci [Internet]. 2020 Jun 28 [cited 2020 Jul 21];10(13):4448. Available from: https://www.mdpi.com/2076-3417/10/13/4448

[29] Bishop CM. Pattern Recognition and Machine Learning (Information Science and Statistics). 1st ed. Springer; 2007.

[30] Ghamisi P, Plaza J, Chen Y, Li J, Plaza AJ. Advanced Spectral Classifiers for Hyperspectral Images: A review. IEEE Geoscience and Remote Sensing Magazine Institute of Electrical and Electronics Engineers Inc.; Mar 1, 2017 p. 8-32.

[31] Vapnik V. Support vector machine. Mach Learn. 1995;20(3):273-97.

[32] Melgani F, Bruzzone L. Classification of hyperspectral remote sensing images with support vector machines. IEEE Trans Geosci Remote Sens. 2004;42(8):1778-90.

[33] Breiman L. Random forests. Mach Learn. 2001;45(1):5-32.

[34] Raczko E, Zagajewski B. Comparison of support vector machine, random forest and neural network classifiers for tree species classification on airborne hyperspectral APEX images. Eur J Remote Sens. 2017 Jan;50(1):144-54.

[35] Böhning D. Multinomial logistic regression algorithm. Ann Inst Stat Math [Internet]. 1992 Mar [cited 2020 Jul 21];44(1):197-200. Available from: https://link.springer.com/article/10.1007/BF00048682

[36] Akbari H, Kosugi Y, Kojima K, Tanaka N. Detection and Analysis of the Intestinal Ischemia Using Visible and Invisible Hyperspectral Imaging. IEEE Trans Biomed Eng. 2010;57(8):2011-7.

[37] Akbari H, Uto K, Kosugi Y, Kojima K, Tanaka N. Cancer detection using infrared hyperspectral imaging. Cancer Sci. 2011 Feb;102(4):852-7.

[38] Akbari H, Halig L V., Schuster DM, Osunkoya A, Master V, Nieh PT, et al. Hyperspectral imaging and quantitative analysis for prostate cancer detection. J Biomed Opt [Internet]. 2012 Jul;17(7):0760051. Available from: http://biomedicaloptics.spiedigitallibrary.org/article.aspx?doi=10.1117/1.JBO.17.7.076005

[39] Liu Z, Wang H, Li Q. Tongue tumor detection in medical hyperspectral images. Sensors [Internet]. 2011;12(1):162-74. Available from: https://www.scopus.com/inward/record.uri?eid=2-s2.0-84863076803&partnerID=40&md5=af7557174562a8e50e3243bcc91cb839

[40] Leon R, Martinez-Vega B, Fabelo H, Ortega S, Melian V, Castaño I, et al. Non-Invasive Skin Cancer Diagnosis Using Hyperspectral Imaging for In-Situ Clinical Support. J Clin Med [Internet]. 2020 Jun 1 [cited 2020 Jul 21];9(6):1662. Available from: https://www.mdpi.com/2077-0383/9/6/1662

[41] Regeling B, Laffers W, Gerstner AOHH, Westermann S, Müller NA, Schmidt K, et al. Development of an image pre-processor for operational

hyperspectral laryngeal cancer detection. J Biophotonics [Internet]. 2016 Mar [cited 2017 May 12];9(3): 235-45. Available from: http://dx.doi.org/10.1002/jbio.201500151

[42] Nakaya D, Tomiyama Y, Satori S, Saegusa M, Yoshida T, Yokoi A, et al. Development of high-performance pathological diagnosis software using a hyperspectral camera. In: 2018 IEEE EMBS Conference on Biomedical Engineering and Sciences, IECBES 2018 - Proceedings. Institute of Electrical and Electronics Engineers Inc.; 2019. p. 217-20.

[43] Ortega S, Fabelo H, Camacho R, de la Luz Plaza M, Callicó GMGM, Sarmiento R, et al. Detecting brain tumor in pathological slides using hyperspectral imaging. Biomed Opt Express [Internet]. 2018 Feb 1;9(2):818-31. Available from: https://www.osapublishing.org/abstract.cfm?URI=boe-9-2-818

[44] Lu G, Little J V., Wang X, Zhang H, Patel MR, Griffith CC, et al. Detection of head and neck cancer in surgical specimens using quantitative hyperspectral imaging. Clin Cancer Res. 2017;23(18):5426-36.

[45] Van Der Maaten LJP, Postma EO, Van Den Herik HJ. Dimensionality Reduction: A Comparative Review. J Mach Learn Res. 2009;10:1-41.

[46] Francis PJ, Wills BJ. Introduction to Principal Components Analysis. PM R [Internet]. 1999 May 6 [cited 2020 Jul 21];6(3):275-8. Available from: http://arxiv.org/abs/astro-ph/9905079

[47] Bruce LM, Koger CH, Li J. Dimensionality reduction of hyperspectral data using discrete wavelet transform feature extraction. IEEE Trans Geosci Remote Sens. 2002 Oct;40(10):2331-8.

[48] Van Der Maaten LJP, Hinton GE. Visualizing high-dimensional data using t-sne. J Mach Learn Res [Internet]. 2008;9:2579-605. Available from: http://www.ncbi.nlm.nih.gov/entrez/query.fcgi?db=pubmed&cmd=Retrieve&dopt=AbstractPlus&list_uids=7911431479148734548related:VOiAgwMNy20J

[49] Deepa SN, Sivanandam SN. Introduction to Genetic Algorithms. In Berlin, Heidelberg: Springer Berlin Heidelberg; 2008. p. 15-37.

[50] Eberhart, Yuhui Shi. Particle swarm optimization: developments, applications and resources. 2002;81-6.

[51] Sun W, Du Q. Hyperspectral band selection: A review. Vol. 7, IEEE Geoscience and Remote Sensing Magazine. Institute of Electrical and Electronics Engineers Inc.; 2019. p. 118-39.

[52] Zuzak KJ, Naik SC, Alexandrakis G, Hawkins D, Behbehani K, Livingston E. Intraoperative bile duct visualization using near-infrared hyperspectral video imaging. Am J Surg. 2008;195(4):491-7.

[53] Wilson JW, Robles FE, Deb S, Warren WS, Fischer MC. Comparison of pump-probe and hyperspectral imaging in unstained histology sections of pigmented lesions. Biomed Opt Express [Internet]. 2017 Aug 1 [cited 2020 Jul 21];8(8):3882. Available from: https://doi.org/10.1364/BOE.8.003882

[54] Halicek M, Fei B, Little J V., Wang X, Patel M, Griffith CC, et al. Optical biopsy of head and neck cancer using hyperspectral imaging and convolutional neural networks. In: Wong BJF, Ilgner JF, Witjes MJ, editors. Optical Imaging, Therapeutics, and Advanced Technology in Head and Neck Surgery and Otolaryngology 2018 [Internet]. SPIE; 2019 [cited 2019 Apr 1]. p. 33. Available from: http://dx.doi.org/10.1117/1.jbo.24.3.036007

[55] Zarei N, Bakhtiari A, Gallagher P, Keys M, Macaulay C. Automated prostate

glandular and nuclei detection using hyperspectral imaging. In: Proceedings - International Symposium on Biomedical Imaging. IEEE Computer Society; 2017. p. 1028-31.

[56] Li Q, Wang Y, Liu H, He X, Xu D, Wang J, et al. Leukocyte cells identification and quantitative morphometry based on molecular hyperspectral imaging technology. Comput Med Imaging Graph. 2014;38(3):171-8.

[57] Fabelo H, Ortega S, Lazcano R, Madroñal D, M. Callicó G, Juárez E, et al. An Intraoperative Visualization System Using Hyperspectral Imaging to Aid in Brain Tumor Delineation. Sensors [Internet]. 2018 Feb 1;18(2):430. Available from: http://www.mdpi.com/1424-8220/18/2/430

[58] Hadoux X, Hui F, Lim JKH, Masters CL, Pébay A, Chevalier S, et al. Non-invasive in vivo hyperspectral imaging of the retina for potential biomarker use in Alzheimer's disease. Nat Commun. 2019 Dec;10(1):1-12.

[59] Ravi D, Fabelo H, Callico GM, Yang GG-Z, Callic GM, Yang GG-Z. Manifold Embedding and Semantic Segmentation for Intraoperative Guidance with Hyperspectral Brain Imaging. IEEE Trans Med Imaging. 2017;36(9).

[60] Ma L, Halicek M, Fei B. In vivo cancer detection in animal model using hyperspectral image classification with wavelet feature extraction. In: Gimi BS, Krol A, editors. Medical Imaging 2020: Biomedical Applications in Molecular, Structural, and Functional Imaging [Internet]. SPIE; 2020 [cited 2020 Jul 21]. p. 48. Available from: https://www.spiedigitallibrary.org/conference-proceedings-of-spie/11317/2549397/In-vivo-cancer-detection-in-animal-model-using-hyperspectral-image/10.1117/12.2549397.full

[61] Pourreza-Shahri R, Saki F, Kehtarnavaz N, Leboulluec P, Liu H. Classification of ex-vivo breast cancer positive margins measured by hyperspectral imaging. In: 2013 IEEE International Conference on Image Processing, ICIP 2013 - Proceedings. 2013. p. 1408-12.

[62] Goto A, Nishikawa J, Kiyotoki S, Nakamura M, Nishimura J, Okamoto T, et al. Use of hyperspectral imaging technology to develop a diagnostic support system for gastric cancer. J Biomed Opt [Internet]. 2015;20(1):016017. Available from: http://biomedicaloptics.spiedigitallibrary.org/article.aspx?doi=10.1117/1.JBO.20.1.016017

[63] Lu G, Wang D, Qin X, Halig L, Muller S, Zhang H, et al. Framework for hyperspectral image processing and quantification for cancer detection during animal tumor surgery. J Biomed Opt [Internet]. 2015;20(12):126012. Available from: http://biomedicaloptics.spiedigitallibrary.org/article.aspx?doi=10.1117/1.JBO.20.12.126012

[64] Martinez B, Leon R, Fabelo H, Ortega S, Piñeiro JF, Szolna A, et al. Most Relevant Spectral Bands Identification for Brain Cancer Detection Using Hyperspectral Imaging. Sensors. 2019 Dec;19(24):5481.

[65] He L, Li J, Liu C, Li S. Recent Advances on Spectral-Spatial Hyperspectral Image Classification: An Overview and New Guidelines. IEEE Trans Geosci Remote Sens. 2018 Mar 1;56(3):1579-97.

[66] Wang Q, Wang J, Zhou M, Li Q, Wang Y, Ang QIANW, et al. Spectral-spatial feature-based neural network method for acute lymphoblastic leukemia cell identification via microscopic hyperspectral imaging technology. Biomed Opt Express. 2017 Jun;8(6).

[67] Li Q, Zhou M, Liu H, Wang Y, Guo F. Red Blood Cell Count

Automation Using Microscopic Hyperspectral Imaging Technology. Appl Spectrosc. 2015 Dec;69(12):1372-80.

[68] Lin L, Zhang S. Superpixel Segmentation of Hyperspectral Images Based on Entropy and Mutual Information. Appl Sci [Internet]. 2020 Feb 13 [cited 2020 Jul 22];10(4):1261. Available from: https://www.mdpi.com/2076-3417/10/4/1261

[69] Fabelo H, Halicek M, Ortega S, Shahedi M, Szolna A, Piñeiro JF, et al. Deep Learning-Based Framework for In Vivo Identification of Glioblastoma Tumor using Hyperspectral Images of Human Brain. Sensors [Internet]. 2019 Feb 22 [cited 2019 Mar 4];19(4):920. Available from: http://www.mdpi.com/1424-8220/19/4/920

[70] Ortega S, Halicek M, Fabelo H, Camacho R, Plaza M de la L, Godtliebsen F, et al. Hyperspectral Imaging for the Detection of Glioblastoma Tumor Cells in H&E Slides Using Convolutional Neural Networks. Sensors. 2020 Mar;20(7):1911.

[71] Halicek M, Dormer JD, Little J V., Chen AY, Myers L, Sumer BD, et al. Hyperspectral Imaging of Head and Neck Squamous Cell Carcinoma for Cancer Margin Detection in Surgical Specimens from 102 Patients Using Deep Learning. Cancers (Basel) [Internet]. 2019 Sep 14 [cited 2019 Nov 17];11(9):1367. Available from: https://www.mdpi.com/2072-6694/11/9/1367

[72] Halicek M, Dormer J, Little J, Chen A, Fei B. Tumor detection of the thyroid and salivary glands using hyperspectral imaging and deep learning. Biomed Opt Express. 2020 Jan;

[73] Halicek M, Little J V., Wang X, Patel MR, Griffith CC, Chen AY, et al. Tumor margin classification of head and neck cancer using hyperspectral imaging and convolutional neural networks. In: Webster RJ, Fei B, editors. Medical Imaging 2018: Image-Guided Procedures, Robotic Interventions, and Modeling [Internet]. SPIE; 2018 [cited 2018 Sep 14]. p. 4. Available from: https://www.spiedigitallibrary.org/conference-proceedings-of-spie/10576/2293167/Tumor-margin-classification-of-head-and-neck-cancer-using-hyperspectral/10.1117/12.2293167.full

[74] TrajanovskiS,ShanC,WeijtmansPJC, de Koning SGB, Ruers TJM. Tumor Semantic Segmentation in Hyperspectral Images using Deep Learning. In: International Conference on Medical Imaging with Deep Learning -- Extended Abstract Track. London, United Kingdom; 2019.

[75] Kho E, Dashtbozorg B, de Boer LL, Van de Vijver KK, Sterenborg HJCM, Ruers TJM. Broadband hyperspectral imaging for breast tumor detection using spectral and spatial information. Biomed Opt Express. 2019 Sep;10(9):4496.

[76] Halicek M, Ortega S, Fabelo H, Lopez C, Lejaune M, Callico GM, et al. Conditional generative adversarial network for synthesizing hyperspectral images of breast cancer cells from digitized histology. In: Tomaszewski JE, Ward AD, editors. Medical Imaging 2020: Digital Pathology [Internet]. SPIE; 2020 [cited 2020 May 22]. p. 29. Available from: https://www.spiedigitallibrary.org/conference-proceedings-of-spie/11320/2549994/Conditional-generative-adversarial-network-for-synthesizing-hyperspectral-images-of-breast/10.1117/12.2549994.full

[77] Bengs M, Gessert N, Laffers W, Eggert D, Westermann S, Mueller NA, et al. Spectral-Spatial Recurrent-Convolutional Networks for In-Vivo Hyperspectral Tumor Type Classification. 2020 Jul;

[78] Li S, Song W, Fang L, Chen Y, Ghamisi P, Benediktsson JA. Deep Learning for Hyperspectral Image Classification: An Overview. IEEE Trans Geosci Remote Sens. 2019;1-20.

Chapter 4

A Hybrid Image Fusion Algorithm for Medical Applications

Appari Geetha Devi, Surya Prasada Rao Borra and Kalapala Vidya Sagar

Abstract

The main objective of medical imaging is to get a extremely informative image for higher designation. One modality of medical image cannot offer correct and complete data in several cases. In brain medical imaging, resonance Imaging (MRI) image shows structural data of the brain with none useful information, wherever as pc imaging (CT) image describes useful data of the brain however with low spatial resolution particularly with low dose CT scan, that is helpful to scale back the radiation impact to physique. Within the field of diagnosing, Image fusion plays a really very important role. Fusing the CT and tomography pictures provides a whole data concerning each soft and exhausting tissues of the physique. This paper proposes a 2 stage hybrid fusion formula. Initial stage deals with the sweetening of a coffee dose CT scan image exploitation totally different image sweetening techniques viz., bar graph Equalization and adaptation bar graph deed. Within the second stage, the improved low dose CT scan image is united with tomography image exploitation totally different fusion algorithms viz., distinct rippling rework (DWT) and Principal element Analysis (PCA). The projected formula has been evaluated and compared exploitation totally different quality metrics.

Keywords: Image fusion, Image Enhancement, MRI Imaging, Low dose CT, DWT, PCA

1. Introduction

In medical imaging, different modalities replicate different details of human organs and tissues. For example, Magnetic Resosance Imaging (MRI) provides low density soft tissues such as blood vessels, whereas Computed Tomography(CT) provides clear detail about bone tissue and also provides the reference for location of the lesion [1]. As it is known, dose reduction lowers the radiation exposure risks, but at the same time decreases the image quality. By its nature, CT involves larger radiation doses than the more common, conventional x-ray imaging procedures [2]. We briefly discuss the nature of CT scanning and its main clinical applications, both in symptomatic patients and, in the screening of asymptomatic patients. We focus on the increasing number of CT scans being obtained, the associated radiation doses, and the consequent cancer risks in adults and particularly in children [3]. Although the risks for any one person are not large, the increasing exposure to radiation in the population may be a public health issue in the future. The use of CT has increased rapidly since 1980's, according to recent surveys, it is showing that

IntechOpen

more than 62 million CT scans are currently obtained ever year in the United States, as compared with about 3 million in 1980's. The largest use of CT scan, however, are within the classes of pediatric identification and adult screening, and these trends are often expected to continue for ensuing few years [4]. The rise in use of CT scan in kids has been driven primarily by the decrease within the time required to scan, that is a smaller amount than a second, and additionally eliminating the necessity for physiological condition to forestall the kid from moving throughout image acquisition method. The foremost growth space in exploitation CT scan for youngsters has been presurgical identification of inflammation, that CT seems to be each correct and efficient.

The radiation doses from CT scanning are considerably larger than those from corresponding conventional radiography. Michael F. McNitt-Gray [3] discussed that the radiation doses to a particular organ from any given CT scan depends on number of factors, such as range of scans, the tube current and scanning time in milliampseconds (mAs), the scale of the patient, the axial scan vary, the scan pitch (the degree of overlap between adjacent CT slices), the tube voltage within the potential unit peaks (kVp), and therefore the specific style of the scanner being employed. Patient dosimetry and evaluation of image quality are basic aspects of any quality control program in diagnostic radiology. Image quality must be adequate for diagnosis and obtained with reasonable patient doses [5]. As per the recommendations of International Commission on Radiological Protection, No dose limit applies to medical exposure to patients, but diagnostic reference levels or reference values have been proposed by the International Commission on Radiologic Protection [6]. Thomas Lehnert et al. said that it is always the relative noise in CT images will increase as the radiation dose decreases, which means that there will always be a tradeoff between the need for low-noise images and the desirability of using low doses of radiation [4]. The low dose CT scan image usually suffers from serious noise and artifacts by using analytical reconstruction methods. It is always preferable to have standard imaging techniques that diminish the patient dose with reasonable image quality [7]. As part of implementation efforts, an important clinical requirement has been addressed that low-dose CT (LDCT) images need to be improved in the Electronic Health Records (EHR). Khalid et al., proposed an enhanced dynamic quadrant equalization for image contrast enhancement, in which input image histogram is divided into 8 subhistograms by using median values. For individual subhistograms, clipping of histogram is done by the average pixels. New dynamic range is assigned to each subhistograms and HE is done separately. This approach preserves the mean brightness [8]. As there is no guarantee that the contrast will always be increased by the histogram equalization [1], Adaptive Histogram Equalisation has been applied on low dose CT scan image to improve the contrast.

This chapter gives a comparative study related to performance of the image fusion techniques. Organization of this paper is as follows; Section 2 explains the image enhancement techniques. The principle of PCA and DWT image fusion techniques are discussed in Section 3. In Section 4, fusion performance assessment techniques are explained. In Section 5, the results of fused images for two different data sets are compared with PCA and DWT applied to medical images by implementing in MATLAB.

2. Image enhancement

The goal of an image enhancement is to improve the visual effects of the entire image or to enhance the certain information in accordance with specific needs [9].

2.1 Histogram equalization

Histogram equalization is a global processing technique used to spread the pixel values over the dynamic range of image and the equalized histogram must be approximately uniformly distributed in the dynamic range [10]. It is a distribution function transformation method based on histogram modification.

Characteristics of Histogram of a digital image:

1. The frequency of the histogram reflects only the pixels in the image of a certain grey level values but not reflects the position of each pixel.

2. Histogram of an image doesn't overlap each sub section of an image.

It is not sure that the contrast will always be increased by the histogram equalization. There may be some cases in which histogram equalization can be worse. In that cases the distinction could also be decreased. In general, normal bar graph exploit uses an equivalent transformation that comes from the image bar graph to rework all pixels. This works well once the distribution of pel values is comparable throughout the image [11]. However, once the image contains regions that square measure considerably lighter or darker than most of the image, the distinction in those regions won't be sufficiently increased. Adaptive bar graph exploit (AHE) improves during this side by remodeling every pel with a change perform derived from its neighbourhood region.

2.2 Adaptive histogram equalization

Adaptive bar graph feat (AHE) may be a pc image process technique wont to improve the distinction in pictures. It differs from normal bar graph feat within the respect that the adaptive technique computes many histograms, every admire a definite section of the image, and uses them to spread the brightness values of the image [12]. In its simplest type, every element is remodeled supported the bar graph of a sq. close that element. The transformation functions derived from the bar graphs is precisely constant as for normal histogram feat. The transformation perform is proportional to the accumulative distribution function (CDF) of element values within the neighbourhood. Pixels close to the image boundary have to be compelled to be treated specially, as a result of their neighbourhood wouldn't lie fully at intervals the image [13]. It is so appropriate for rising the native distinction and enhancing the definitions of edges in every region of a picture. However, AHE contains a tendency to over amplify noise in comparatively homogeneous regions of a picture. Properties of Adaptive Histogram Equalisation:

- The size of the neighbourhood region is a parameter of the method. It improves the contrast at smaller scales and reduces the contrast at larger scales.

- Due to the character of bar chart feat, the resultant price of a component underneath AHE is proportional to its rank among the pixels in its neighbourhood. This permits Associate in Nursing economical implementation of hardware that may compare the middle component with all different pixels within the neighbourhood [3]. Associate in Nursing unnormalized result price may be computed by adding two for every component with a smaller price than the middle component, and adding one for every component with equal price.

- When the image region containing a pixel's neighbourhood that is uniform, its bar graph are going to be powerfully peaked, and therefore the transformation perform can map a slender vary of constituent values to the complete vary of the resultant image [14]. This causes AHE to over amplify the little amounts of noise in for the most part uniform regions of the image [4].

3. Image fusion

3.1 DWT image fusion

Image fusion process is used to associate the two or more images in to a single image. The resultant fused image obtained will be more explanatory than the distinct source images. The wave remodel may be a mathematical tool which will be wont to discover native options in an exceedingly signal method. It can also be wont to decompose two-dimensional (2D) signals like second grayscale image signals into totally different resolution levels for multiresolution analysis. Wave remodel has been greatly utilized in several areas, like information compression, texture analysis, feature detection, and image fusion.

Wavelet transforms offer a framework within which a picture is rotten, with every level equivalent to lower band and better frequency bands. The DWT may be a spatial-frequency decomposition that provides a versatile multiresolution analysis of a picture. In general, the essential plan of image fusion supported ripple remodel is to perform a multiresolution decomposition on every supply image; the coefficients of each the low-frequency band and high-frequency bands are then performed with a definite fusion rule [13]. The wide used fusion rule is most choice rule. This straightforward theme simply selects the biggest absolute ripple constant at every location from the input pictures because the constant at that location within the united image [15]. After that, the united image is obtained by playacting the inverse DWT (IDWT) for the corresponding combined ripple coefficients. The elaborated fusion steps supported ripple remodel will be summarized below.

Step 1. the pictures to be amalgamated should be registered to assure that the corresponding pixels square measure aligned.

Step 2. These pictures square measure rotten into riffle remodeled pictures, severally, supported riffle transformation. The remodeled pictures with K-level decomposition can embrace one low-frequency portion (low-low band) and three high-frequency parts (low-high bands, poker game bands, and high-high bands).

Step 3. The remodel coefficients of various parts or bands square measure performed with an explicit fusion rule.

Step 4. The amalgamated image is built by acting associate inverse riffle remodel supported the combined remodel coefficients from Step 3 [16].

The overall fusion processing goes through the preprocessing and image registration followed by wavelet decomposition. The input images must be of same size for fusion. For easy computation and to abstract data, the image has got to be born-again into a grey scaled image from color image. Bar chart standardisation provides tonal distribution of the complete image. Preprocessed pictures square measure split in to four frequency sub bands like LL, LH, HL and HH. A general fusion rule is to select, the coefficients whose values are higher and the more dominant features at each scale are preserved in the new multi-resolution representation [17]. The fused image is constructed by performing an inverse wavelet transformation. The main objective of an image fusion is combining complimentary, as well as redundant data from multiple pictures to make one image that provides a lot of complete and correct description. This amalgamated image is a lot of appropriate for human visual, machine perception or additional image process and analysis tasks. Another advantage of image fusion is that it decreases the cupboard space and price by storing solely the one amalgamated image, rather than storing totally different modality pictures [14]. within the space of medical imaging, combining the photographs {of totally different| of various} modalities of same scene offers numerous benefits it should be fusion of image taken at different spatial resolution, intensity and by totally different strategies helps medical practitioner/Radiologists to simply extract or acknowledge the options or abnormalities that will not be typically visible in single image [18] (**Figure 1**).

3.1.1 Simple averaging rule

In remodel primarily based fusion formula an easy "averaging rule" is adopted to fuse the low frequency coefficients. Low-frequency coefficients contain define data associated with the image rather than specific major details, ANd therefore an averaging technique is applied to provide the composite low-frequency coefficients [18]. The computation is performed as follows:

$$F(x,y) = \frac{F_1(x,y) + F_2(x,y)}{2} \tag{1}$$

where F(x, y) are the low frequency coefficients of the fused image IF, f_1(x, y) and f_2(x, y) are the low frequency coefficients of the source images.

3.1.2 Maximum selection rule

Maximum selection rule is used in high frequency coefficients. Two images wavelet coefficients are compared and select the maximum value coefficient for fusion process as shown in Eq. (2)

$$W(x,y) = \begin{matrix} W_1(X,Y) & \text{if } I_1(x,y) > I_2(x,y) \\ W_2(X,Y) & \text{if } I_1(x,y) < I_2(x,y) \end{matrix} \tag{2}$$

W_1 (x, y) – Image l wavelet coefficient.
W_2 (x, y) - Image 2 wavelet coefficient.

3.2 Principal component analysis

Principal element analysis is performed that aims at decreasing giant an outsized an oversized set of variables into a little set that also containing most of the data that

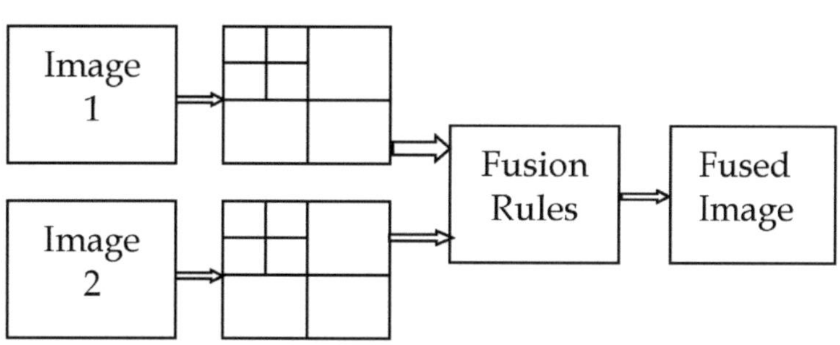

Figure 1.
Fusion Process using Wavelet transforms.

was existing within the large set. As medical image knowledge is large, to cut back these knowledge PCA methodology is important. The strategy of principal element analysis permits USA to make and use a weakened set of variables, that area unit referred to as principal vectors. A reduced set is way easier to research and interpret. The foremost simple thanks to build a amalgamate image of many input pictures is playing the fusion as a weighted superposition of all input images [14]. The best coefficient coefficients, with relevancy info content and redundancy removal, is determined by a principal element analysis (PCA) of all input intensities. By computing PCA of the variance matrix of input intensities, the weights for every input image area unit obtained from the eigenvector comparable to the most important chemist price. PCA is that the simplest of verity eigenvector-based statistical procedure. Often, its operation is thought of as revealing the interior structure of the information in a very means that best explains the variance within the data [19]. If a variable knowledge set is envisioned as a collection of coordinates in a very high-dimensional data area (1 axis per variable), PCA will offer the user with a lower-dimensional image, a "shadow" of this object once viewed from its most informative viewpoint. This can be done by mistreatment solely the primary few principal parts in order that the spatial property of the remodeled knowledge is reduced. The amount of principal parts is a smaller amount than or capable the amount of original variables [20].

PCA Algorithm:

- Transform the info into column vectors. Confirm the mean on every column
- Subtract the empirical mean vector.
- Compute the variance matrix C of X i.e. =XXT
- Mean of expectation = covariance(X).
- Compute the eigenvectors V and Eigen|chemist} price D of C and kind them by decreasing Eigen price
- Consider the primary column of V that corresponds to larger Eigen price to figure P1 and P2 as
- P1 = V(1)/ΣV and P2 = V(2)/ΣV

The input images (images to be fused) $I_1(x, y)$ and $I_2(x, y)$ are arranged in two column vectors and their empirical means are subtracted. From the resulting vector, compute the eigenvector and Eigen values and the Eigenvectors corresponding to the larger eigen value are obtained. The normalized components P_1 and P_2 (i.e., $P_1 + P_2 = 1$) are computed from the obtained eigenvector. The fused image is

$$I_F(x,y) = P_1 * I_1(x,y) + P_2 * I_2(x,y) \tag{3}$$

Where P_1 and P_2 are the principal components.

4. Performance analysis

In this, the outcome of fusion transformation is evaluated with different parameter, may be quantitatively & qualitatively and compared the results with the other algorithms, to check efficiency of the hybrid algorithm. Some of the quantitative parameters are listed below:

Entropy: Entropy is a measure of the information content in an image. An image with high information will have high entropy.

$$H = -\sum_{i=0}^{L-1} p_i \log(p_i) \tag{4}$$

Where L is the number of grey levels in an image; P_i is the probability of occurring i^{th} grey level.

Standard Deviation: Standard Deviation is used to measure the contrast in the fused image. It consists of both signal and noise, an image with more information would have high standard deviation.

$$\sigma = \sqrt{\sum_{i=0}^{L-1} (i - \bar{i})^2 h_{If}(i)} \tag{5}$$

Where $h_{If}(i)$ is the normalized histogram of the fused image; L is the number of grey levels in an image.

Mean Squared Error:

$$MSE = \frac{\sum_{i=0}^{M-1}\sum_{j=0}^{N-1}[R(i,j) - F(i,j)]^2}{MXN} \tag{6}$$

Root Mean Square Error (RMSE): The error between fused image F and reference image R is given by,

$$RMSE = \sqrt{\frac{\sum_{i=0}^{M-1}\sum_{j=0}^{N-1}[R(i,j) - F(i,j)]^2}{MXN}} \tag{7}$$

Where R is reference image and F is fused image.

Peak Signal-to-Noise Ratio (PSNR):

PSNR is the ratio between the maximum possible power of a signal and the power of corrupting noise that affects the fidelity of its representation.

The PSNR measure is given by

$$PSNR = 10 * \log_{10} \frac{(L-1)^2}{MSE} \tag{8}$$

The higher the PSNR value, better the fusion process.

5. Results and discussion

The proposed algorithms are tested and compared with different fusion techniques. The testing data sets are of two medical modality images like, CT and MRI of size 480X403. The original MRI image of set 1 is shown in **Figure 2(a)** and also the CT image of set 1 is shown in **Figure 2(b)**.

Figure 3 shows an image resulting from DWT simple averaging fusion technique. DWT maximum selection rule is applied on data set 1 and resulting image is shown in **Figures 4** and **5** shows an image which is obtained from PCA fusion method.

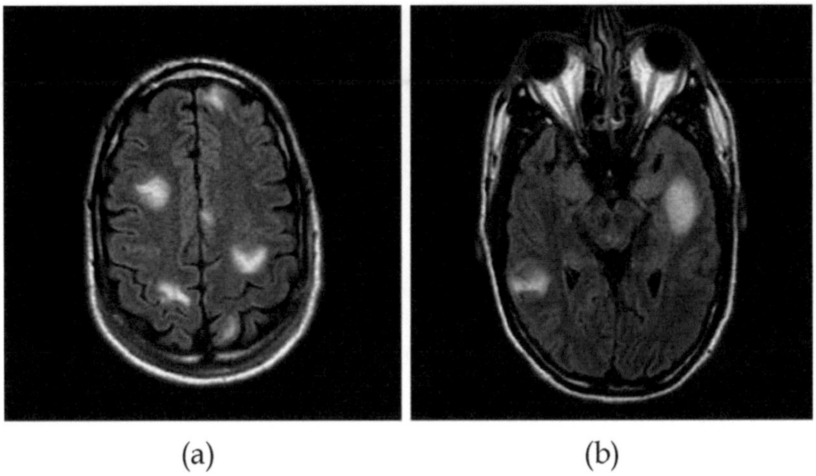

Figure 2.
Data set-1 of the brain. (a) MRI scan image. (b) CT scan image.

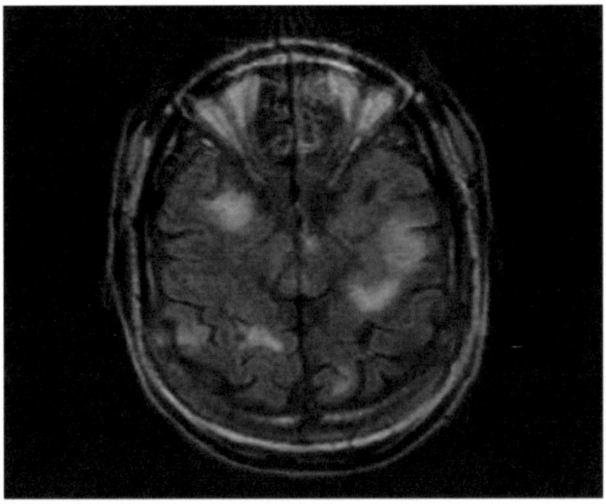

Figure 3.
Fused image of data set 1 in DWT. Simple Averaging method.

Table 1 shows the values of different quality parametric measures like Entropy, Standard Deviation, Mean Squared Error and Root Mean Squared Error for various fusion algorithms. Values for the proposed PCA is resulted better than other w.r.t the quality parametric measures.

The testing data sets are of two medical modality images i.e., CT and MRI of size 410X388. The original MRI image of set 2 is shown in **Figure 6(a)** and the CT image of set 1 is shown in **Figure 6(b)**.

DWT maximum selection rule is applied on data set 2 and resulting image is shown in **Figures 7** and **8** shows an image resulting from DWT simple averaging fusion technique and **Figure 9** shows an image which is obtained from PCA fusion method.

Table 2 shows, the values of different quality parametric measures like Entropy, Standard Deviation, Mean Squared Error and Root Mean Squared Error for various fusion algorithms. Values for the proposed PCA is resulted better than other w.r.t the quality parametric measures.

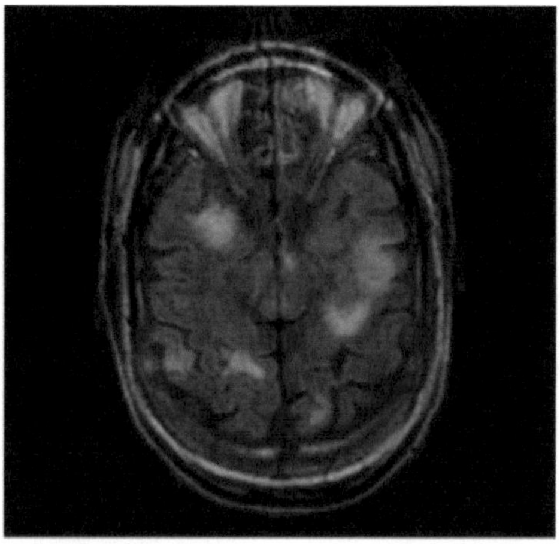

Figure 4.
Fused image of data set 1 in DWT. Maximum selection Rule method.

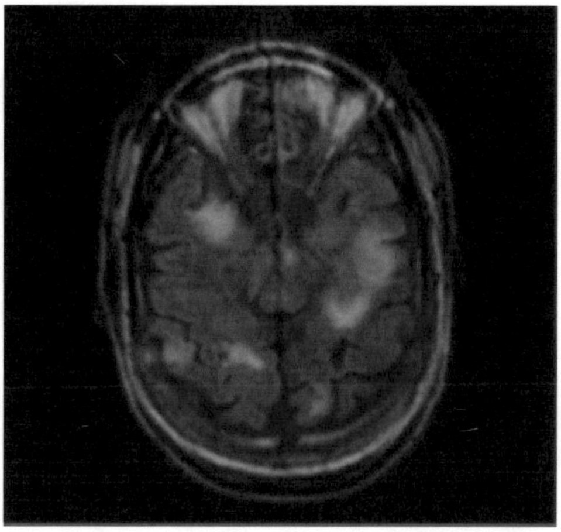

Figure 5.
Fused image of data set-1 in PCA.

	DWT Simple Averaging				
	Entropy	**Standard Deviation**	**MSE**	**RMSE**	**PSNR**
CT	4.5208	74.0343			
MRI	5.6829	73.4328			
DWT Simple Average	5.8438	71.2463	91.2320	9.5515	47.3835
DWT Maximum Selection Rule	6.2348	69.3433	94.0791	9.6994	53.3932
PCA	**7.0439**	**67.3869**	**95.2059**	**9.7573**	**58.6465**
Existing [20]	6.9253	66.8564	96.6523	9.3254	56.3254

Table 1.
Comparison parameters of the output images of fusion algorithm of Dataset-1.

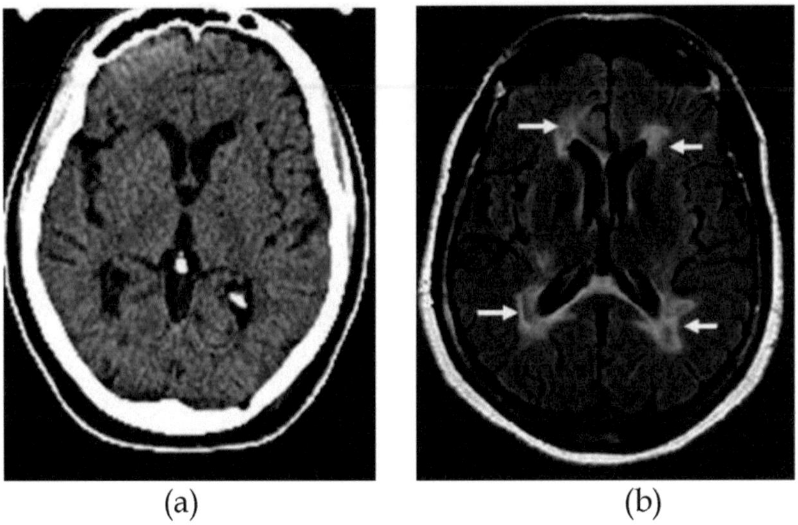

Figure 6.
Data set-2 of the brain. (a) MRI scan image. (b) CT scan image.

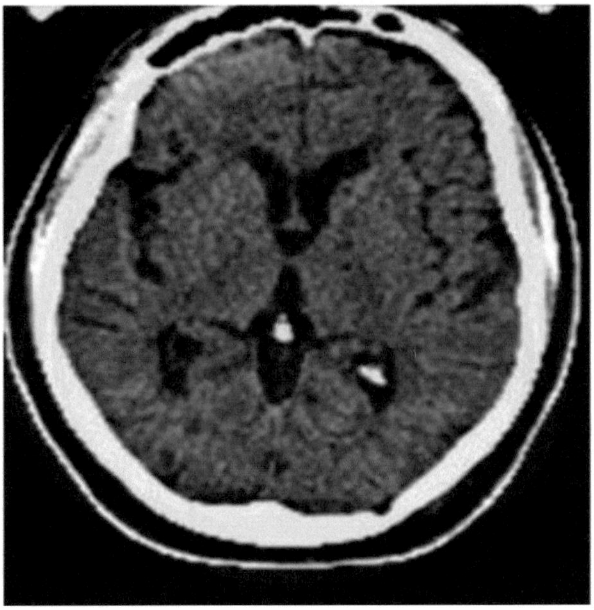

Figure 7.
Fused image of data set 2 in DWT. Maximum selection Rule method.

6. Conclusion

Image fusion plays a very important role in medical diagnosis to help doctors for examining the abnormalities in CT and MRI images. In this chapter, different image fusion techniques have been discussed and three algorithms have been implemented in MATLAB for two different datasets collected from various sources

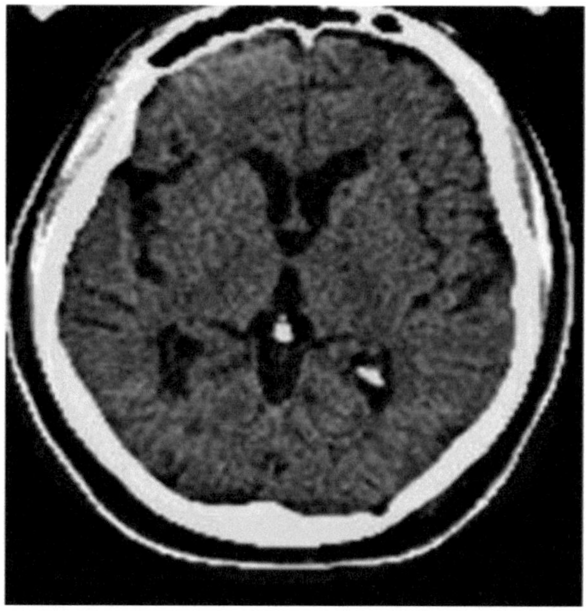

Figure 8.
Fused image of Data set-2 in DWT. Simple Averaging Method.

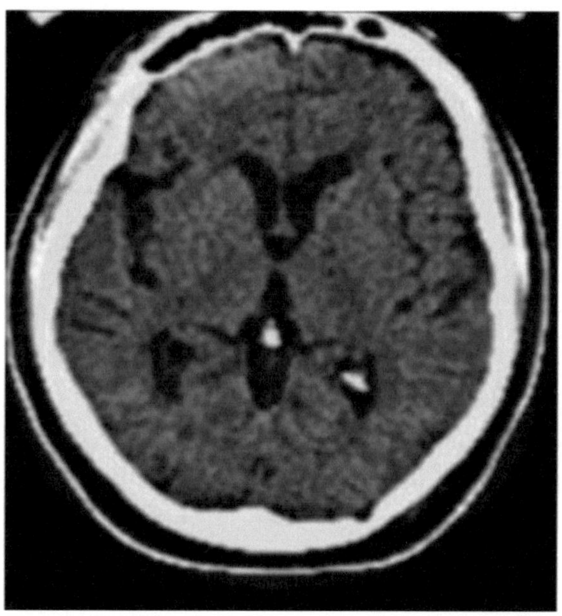

Figure 9.
Fused image of data set-2 in PCA.

and compared the results with the existing methods in literature. Low dose CT scan images have been enhanced using Image enhancement techniques and fused with MRI images. From the results, it is analysed that the PCA algorithm results in better performance in terms of PSNR, MSE and RMSE.

	DWT Maximum Selection Rule				
	Entropy	**Standard Deviation**	**MSE**	**RMSE**	**PSNR**
CT	6.3425	81.1017	—	—	—
MRI	5.6423	53.3808	—	—	—
DWT Simple Average	6.6093	73.5183	99.8073	9.9904	28.1394
DWT Maximum Selection Rule	6.6746	72.3431	78.7480	8.8740	29.1684
PCA	**6.6921**	**70.2923**	**72.0784**	**8.4899**	**29.5528**
Existing [20]	6.6235	69.6541	70.3512	7.6854	28.3522

Table 2.
Comparison parameters of the output images of fusion algorithm of Dataset-2.

Author details

Appari Geetha Devi[1], Surya Prasada Rao Borra[1*] and Kalapala Vidya Sagar[2]

1 Prasad V. Potluri Siddhartha Institute of Technology, Kanuru, Vijayawada, Andhra Pradesh, India

2 VNR Vignana Jyothi Institute of Engineering and Technology, Hyderabad, India

*Address all correspondence to: suryaborra1679@gmail.com

References

[1] Surya Prasada Rao Borra, Rajesh K Panakala and P, Rajesh Kumar, "Qualitative Anlysis of MRI and Enhanced Low Dose CT scan Image Fusion", International Conference on Advanced Computing and Communication Systems (ICACCS - 2017), Jan. 06 – 07, 2017, Coimbatore, INDIA, pp. 1752-1757

[2] David J. Brenner and Eric J. Hall, "Computed Tomography — An Increasing Source of Radiation Exposure", The new engl and journal of medicine

[3] Michael F. McNitt-Gray, "AAPM/ RSNA Physics Tutorial for Residents: Topics in CT - Radiation Dose in CT", Volume 22, Number 6, pp. 1541-1553.

[4] Thomas Lehnert, Nagy N.N. Naguib, Huedayi Korkusuz, Ralf W. Bauer, J. Matthias Kerl, Martin G. Mack, Thomas J. Vogl, Image-Quality Perception asa Function of Dose in Digital Radiography

[5] Eliseo Vano, Jose I Ten, Jose M. Fernandez-Soto and Roberto M. Sanchez-Casanueva, "Experience With Patient Dosimetry and Quality Control Online for Diagnostic and Interventional Radiology Using DICOM Services", Medical Physics and Informatics- Review, AJR: 200, April 2013, pp. 783-790.

[6] Mona Selim, Hiroyuki Kudo and Essam A. Rashed, "Low-Dose CT Image Reconstruction Method WithProbabilistic Atlas Prior", 978-1-4673-9862-6/15/©2015 IEEE.

[7] Nithyananda C R, Ramachandra A C and Preethi, "Survey on Histogram Equalization method based Image Enhancement techniques," 2016 International Conference on Data Mining and Advanced Computing (SAPIENCE), Ernakulam, 2016, pp. 150-158.

[8] J. M. Headlee, E. J. Balster and W. F. Turri, "A no-reference image enhancement quality metric and fusion technique," 2015 International Conference on Image and Vision Computing New Zealand (IVCNZ), Auckland, 2015, pp. 1-6.

[9] D. S. Gowri and T. Amudha, "A Review on Mammo gram Image Enhancement Techniques for Breast Cancer Detection," 2014 International Conference on Intelligent Computing Applications, Coimbatore, 2014, pp. 47-51.

[10] S. S. Jarande, P. K. Kadbe and A. W. Bhagat, "Compartive analysis of image enhancement techniques," 2016 International Conference on Electrical, Electronics, and Optimization Techniques (ICEEOT), Chennai, 2016, pp. 4586-4588.

[11] A.S. Sekhar and M.N.G. Prasad, "A novel approach of image fusion on MR and CT images using wavelet transforms", 2011 3rd International Conference on Electronics Computer Technology, Kanyakumari, 2011, pp. 172-176.

[12] K. Parmar and Kher, "A Comparative Analysis of Multimodality Medical Image Fusion Methods", Sixth Asia Modelling Symposium, Bali, 2012, pp. 93-97.

[13] Jinwen Yang, Weihe Zhong and Zheng Miao, "On the Image enhancement histogram processing", 2016 3rd International conference on informative and Cybernetics for Computational Social Systems (ICCSS), Jinzhou, 2016, pp. 252-255.

[14] P. Mathiyalagan, "Multi-Modal Medical Image Fusion Using Curvelet Algorithm", Advances in Computing Communications and Informatics (ICACCI) 2018 International Conference on, pp. 2453-2458, 2018.

[15] M.D. Nandeesh and Dr. M. Meenakshi, "Image Fusion Algorithms for medical Images – A comparison, Bonfring", International Journal of Advances in Image Processing, Vol. 5, No. 3, July 2015, pp. 23-26.

[16] Vani M and Saravanakumar S, "Multi focus and multi modal image fusion using wavelet transform", 2015 3rd International Conference on Signal Processing, Communication and Networking (ICSCN), Chennai, 2015, pp. 1-6.

[17] Q. Li, J. Du, F. Song, C. Wang, H. Liu and C. Lu, "Region based multi-focus image fusion using the local spatial frequency", 2013 25th Chinese Control and Decision Conference (CCDC), Guiyang, 2013, pp. 3792-3796.

[18] V. Amala Rani, S. Lalithakumari, "A Hybrid Fusion Model for Brain Tumor Images of MRI and CT", Communication and Signal Processing (ICCSP) 2020 International Conference on, pp. 1312-1316, 2020.

[19] Lilia Lazli, Mounir Boukadoum, Otmane Ait Mohamed, "A Survey on Computer-Aided Diagnosis of Brain Disorders through MRI Based on Machine Learning and Data Mining Methodologies with an Emphasis on Alzheimer Disease Diagnosis and the Contribution of the Multimodal Fusion", Applied Sciences, vol. 10, pp. 1894, 2020.

[20] Jiayin Kang, Wu Lu, Wenjuan Zhang, "Fusion of Brain PET and MRI Images Using Tissue-Aware Conditional Generative Adversarial Network With Joint Loss", Access IEEE, vol. 8, pp. 6368-6378, 2020.

Section 3

Forensic Multimedia Retrieval Techniques

Chapter 5

The Role of Penetration Testing in Forensic Multimedia Retrieval Process

Amr Adel and Brian Cusack

Abstract

Digital forensic investigators are faced with multimedia retrieval and discovery challenges that require innovation and application of evolving methodologies. This work is made more difficult in critical infra-structure environments where the acquired evidence is in many formats, types and presentations. Penetration testing is one of the techniques used to focus an investigation and to target the potential case information from the vulnerability identification phase, through to the media identification phase. In this chapter a review of these processes is made and a framework example developed to show how the investigator discovers relevant evidence. The problem for the digital investigator is the vast array of media in which evidence is stored or transmitted. Some work is from live retrieval and others static. A framework of methods that is flexible and adaptable to the context of investigation is proposed and the discovery methods for multimedia environments elaborated.

Keywords: penetration testing, digital forensics, critical infrastructures, evidence extraction, process framework

1. Introduction

Forensic Investigators conduct forensic examinations in order to identify evidence and to prevent future compromises of a system. The increasing volume of digital data to be managed and the diversity of media type is a contemporary challenge. The diversity of devices, operating systems, media and services present obstacles that require solution for efficient and effective professional practice. The variety of data sources, formats and styles poses a multimedia problem that requires working solutions for information access and content documentation. The acquired evidence can include different types of forensic data such as pictures, audios, videos, files, directories, and texts [1]. The systems for extraction are either live and functioning or static and stored. In either situation due processes, methods, standards and guidelines must be complied to achieve a repeatable practice for later auditing. In many instances copies are taken of the various media so analysis proceeds on identical images and not the original media. Investigation processes are segregated into phases to assure the best deployment of specialist skills and the preservation of the evidence [2]. Segregation is usually divided into preparation, acquisition, analysis, and reporting phases and sequenced towards a deliverable that provides corrective actions [3]. In such a situation the system of work and the targeting of the work objectives are critical to the deliverable and the viability of an investigation. In this Chapter we derive a framework for investigation in an intensive multimedia environment and then demonstrate the targeting power of penetration testing techniques.

Critical infrastructures (CI) involve complex systems for the control and protection of assets, and the production and distribution of services to detect suspicious activities [4]. Any unplanned disturbance to these facilities seriously affects the quality of life and economic wellbeing of humans. Modern society depends on digital infrastructures to provide their management of services and the fair and timely distribution. For example, one day of disrupted power supply to a region of users stops work of all kinds and prevents the usual activities that support daily living [5]. Extended power failure causes long-term destruction of economic relationships and negatively affects the necessities for daily life. These systems require protection and one of the ways to do this is to use forensic investigation of events, and to do penetration testing before anything unplanned occurs [6]. In addition to other security provisions, forensic techniques are commonly implemented to document baseline configurations in order to detect abnormal activities, such as unauthorized access into network infrastructure. However, the challenge is to gain a fair estimation of the data provisions in the systems that are chaotically fill of large volumes of static and live data, and a full range of multimedia data types [7].

In this research we designed and tested an investigation framework for multimedia data types to address the challenges of evidence collection in CIs. The volume and complexity issues influence the evidence collection phase but also each environment has unique features from organizational cultures, administration designs, recovery tools, record structures, logging systems, and general usage patterns that all impact the scope and success of an investigation [8]. In addition, there are further challenges such as automation, volatility of data, and data mingling. Automation creates key information resources in order to handle the data and abstract data from its context. Volatility makes the process of collecting data difficult because the data within the collection process is removed, deleted, or overwritten [9]. Furthermore, Data Mingling is a serious problem of data mixing and the types being indistinguishable. Often, the sample of total data investigated in the forensic process comprises of both data related to the incident and data unrelated to the incident [10]. Forensic investigators require help to make sense of the complex multimedia contexts in which they have to work. An investigation framework that is responsive to CI complexities and has targeting features to make workloads manageable is required. The following sections describe how these requirements are designed and become functional in an investigation process.

2. Background literature

Industrial Control Systems in critical infrastructures support monitoring, administering, and controlling essential services. Therefore, by design architecture, components, and environments in CI, allow forensic capabilities to be implemented and to further mitigate the potential risk of security failure. Industrial Control System Architecture is deployed based on Service Oriented Architecture [11]. Hence, three different designs are found according to the architecture of the system. First, Supervisory Control and Data Acquisition (SCADA) systems apply central administration by using a central computer to communicate remotely through a Remote Terminal Unit (RTU). A Human Machine Interface (HCI) is linked to SCADA and facilitates the process of displaying, and monitoring processes. The typical uses

Level	Information System	Media Type
0	Sensor Networks, Internet of Things, and so on	Data, streams of text and digits
1	Programmable Logic Controller, Picture Archiving and Communication	Structured data, text, frames, objects
2	Supervisory Control and Data Acquisition	Ladder logics, objects, words, text and digits
3	Management Expert and Management Information Systems	Images, videos, text, files, directories
4	Enterprise Resource Planning	Files, directories, all manner of media type

Table 1.
CI Media types at organization levels.

for SCADA are in natural gas, electricity, and water distribution [12]. Second, Distributed Control Systems (DCS) distribute processes that have been controlled to devices for execution [13]. The typical uses of DCS are in manufacturing, chemical and electric power plants. Third, Non-Centralised System design allows for a number of control systems that do not require centralised administration. Accordingly, Programmable Logic Controllers (PLC) or any other control devices can be implemented and configured as a combination of Control System, Data Historian and Human Machine Interface [13]. This type of configuration is usually designed for manufacturing processes.

The distribution of media type is found spread evenly through the layers of an industrial control system for CI [14]. These layers are often described as starting at layer 0 where the sensors of the system and primitive data are found, through to layer 4 which is the enterprise level where the business applications and rich media reside [15]. In **Table 1** these layers and media types are described and elaborated to identify the data types and the diversity of media type a digital investigator must review in discovery processes. Discovery processes hence require extreme multimedia processing capabilities that can span the scope of data type and format found in a CI environment. This requires critical tool selection and the designing of staged and sequenced tool use for comprehensive discovery. The task is difficult and is challenged by the constant innovation and adoption of new data type and structures that come with new versions of software and new applications. The multimedia processing capability an investigator chooses reflects the design and scope of an investigation, and the professional capacity to adapt and acquire the necessary tools and techniques [16, 17].

3. Designing a framework

Primarily an investigator requires a systematized process framework to effectively guide an investigation through the known and unknown media types found in a CI investigation. The design proceeds through a phased approach outlined in **Figure 1**. A digital forensic investigation in engineering workstations or control rooms in CIs includes all electronic devices that are interconnected with each other for sending/receiving messages or two-way communications, such as, mobile phones, laptops, computers, tablets, PDAs, programmable logic controllers, human machine interfaces, and supervisory control and data acquisition systems [16]. These systems and devices have their own storage systems. Either physical storage systems or virtual technologies such as cloud computing for logging all activities, incidents, and events [18–21]. Conducting a forensic investigation on engineering

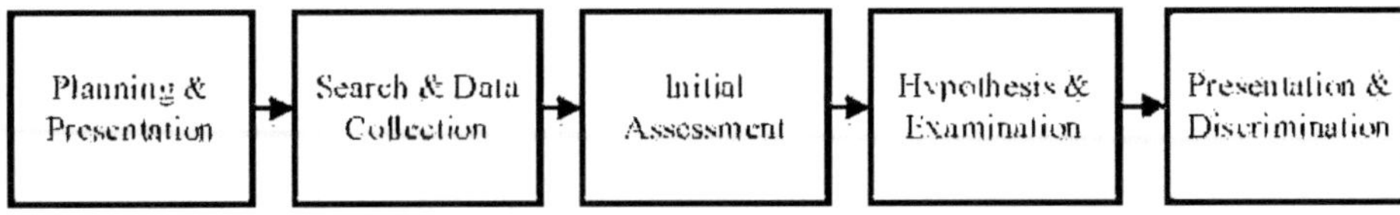

Figure 1.
The Five Phases.

workstations and applying physical and remote data acquisition will discover evidence in the different media that can be used for legal, employment, and other purposes [22]. In this type of investigation, physical and remote data acquisition are an advantage, and hence the investigation equipment must have the capacity to manage volumes, data complexities and multimedia types.

Each investigation requires phases that develop the focus for evidence collection and then pass the findings to the next phase for further refinement. Planning and Identification is a starting point for a structured investigation. At this stage, the incident has to be verified in order to collect fact sheets and plan for a capability handling strategy for the particular case. The major objective of this phase is to boost the productivity of gathering the necessary information about the incident and facilitate the process of data acquisition [23]. Critically the acceptance of multimedia types by the acquisition tools allows credibility to be established and documented against the brief scope. If media types cannot be collected then the performance and adequacy of the investigation are brought into question. Furthermore, obtaining authorizations and authentications are also compulsory, when the case needs an authorized access to the system for media acquisition. System settings are one of most important facts required to be obtained by investigators for determining the device's system state when the incident occurred. System settings can include the system specifications of all machines that are under investigation, and the time or date. Moreover, conducting a network reconnaissance is the last step to obtain IP addresses of all machines and their mac addresses and any other information that could lead to personal ownership identification or related activities [23]. At each of the context levels in **Table 1** different evidence is located and each data and media type must be accommodated in the framework design.

The search and data collection stage employs discovery techniques that allow all information in the multiplicity of media types present to be collected. The investigation process requires detailed information about the daily events for the users in the systems and machines or devices. All information that is collected, will be taken into consideration and preserved for relevancy determination. The collected data goes in to a complex process to determine whether the data acquired is compliant to evidentiary standards and the acquisition process and the deliverable are reproducible by others. If the data is admissible, then it will go to further analysis for case relevancy and positioning in the data log. If not, the data will be stored for a specific period of time and reserved for analysis later when the circumstances may have changed. This stage aims to prepare all potential credible data to go through a parsing process, which is a more detailed analysis and sieving of the data. All necessary data is available to construct and to reconstruct a walkthrough of the control room.

A penetration testing phase is useful to target and to identify weaknesses in the system under investigation [24]. It is conducted remotely for acquiring live data on the system often when the users have not been formally informed that their machines are going through forensic investigation [25]. This step will assist in preserving live data before the digital evidence gets damaged or corrupted. The aim of this step is to combat the anti-forensic tools used by advanced persistent threat (APT) attackers and professional hackers in critical infrastructures [26]. Dead or static acquisition will be confirmed as the second step when relevant evidence is found. At this step, screenshots can be taken as a credible evidence of weaknesses and potential vulnerabilities to the work system.

The data examination stage features methodical assessment of all data, fact sheets, system settings, parsed data, data that came from the initial assessment, and media. Further processes of data analysis and examination also assure each media type is correctly processed and tools are found to process any irregular types. Timeline analysis and other perspectives allow systematic categorization and documentation of the relevant elements of information for the case [27]. This is a vital stage and beneficial as it comprises evidence history such as what time the files have been accessed, modified, created and changed, in a clear format that humans can understand. The data is collected using a diversity of applications and is released from the layer of metadata from the file system regardless of the operating system or format, and then analyzed. The timeline is fixed and application data reconstructed if required as a part of the data analysis and examination. Media and artefact analyses is addressed by, for example, what applications have been executed, which archives have been opened or downloaded, which documents have been clicked on, which records were checked, which files were deleted, where did the user browse, and many other properties. Another type of analysis, which is necessary for finding indirect paths of information is at the signature level. This analysis is where forensic investigators implement techniques and practices that will search for byte signatures of known folders, files and regular expressions that lead to the cookies. Link analysis is employed to find the relationships and trusted links to other entities, servers, domains, email, images, audio, people, and other relevant objects that can be traced to identify all possible communications [28].

Finally reporting and presentation is the stage that contains reporting the results of the analysis and then presenting it to requested recipients. This step includes stating potential risks, clarifying the actions taken, specifying what other arrangements are required for completion; also suggestions for enhancing procedures, guidelines, policies, applications, and other aspects of the forensic process investigations required in the target infrastructure [29]. This step is essential as it is important for the stakeholders in order to determine what strategies they must think about for future preparation. It includes a capability statement with respect to the investigation ability to process all multimedia formats or otherwise. The report has to be formulated in a form that is acceptable to the court or for any legal, employment or administrative purpose.

4. The framework

Digital forensic investigation frameworks have typically been developed for specialist areas of investigation by selecting standardized and repeatable process steps. In the former section we have described such phased steps for the generation of an investigation guideline for CI. However, what has yet to be addressed is the unique system and architectures of CI designs. A CI divides into work stations and control rooms. These are the two areas in which evidence must be collected by an investigator. The workstations interface at each of the CI levels described in Section 2 and **Table 1** and carry live data and stored data that can include volatile components such as RAMs and Flash memory. The digital investigator has to strategically plan for the full range of devices and media types, and to tactically deploy capability to act effectively and efficiently in these environments. The digital investigator is also faced with enormous volumes of data and not just the variability of formats. To cope with volumes our modelling proposes deployment of Hadoop architectures to manage the big data volumes, and the selection of relevant evidences. **Figure 2** is designed to include these features and to deliver sufficient guidance to a digital investigator that they can manage the challenges of a CI environment. The framework provides control of the investigation from the five central phases where each phase appropriately connects to the big data issues on the right, and the workstation and control room issues on the left.

4.1 The five phases of investigation

The framework design centers the five phases of digital investigation between the two challenges in the CI environment – the media complexity and the data volumes. An investigator proceeds through the five phases described in Section 3 to assure completion and compliance with standardized procedures. The systematic and sequenced approach allows concentration on the system in focus and the completion of the professional activities associated. The investigator has the deliverable and the budget in mind at all times. Different types of evidence require different treatment and handling while data format and media type determine adequate access for imaging. By staging the investigation phases in the center of the framework the work system is established and the challenges of the environment are managed, phase by phase. On the left hand side the complexities of the CI workstation context and on the right hand side the strategy for managing large data quantities, are specified. The investigator can hence branch left and right to effectively acquire evidence, while maintaining the phased requirements for due processes.

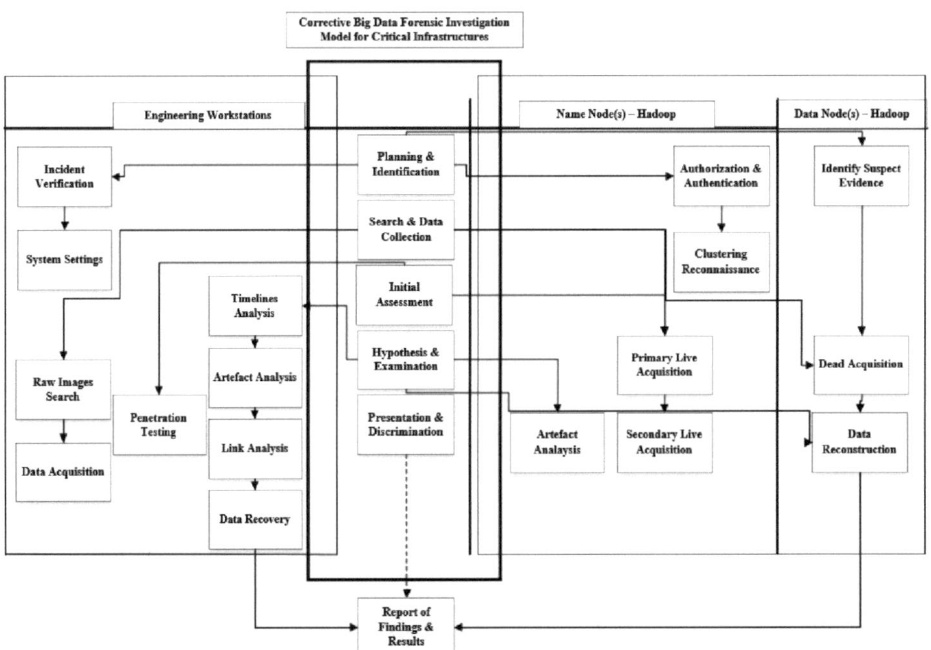

Figure 2.
A CI Investigation Framework.

4.2 Workstation and control room investigation

The workstations and control rooms context requires structured and planned entry. The control for investigation comes from the central digital investigation phases and the management constraints. At any step acquired evidence can include different types of forensic data such as pictures, audios, videos, text, files, directories, and so on. The multi layered challenge of the environment has to be addressed by strategy and tools that have proven effectiveness for data identification, time matching, multi-tenancy acquisition, data ownership differentiation, live forensic acquisition, privacy and privilege compliance, operating systems variation, media variation, format variations, and cloud compatibility. Sophisticated tools such as those that copy processes, examine evidence, analyze programs for generating checksums in order to complete the verification may not fit perfectly to some of control systems technologies. Control system technologies are also time stamped by the history of the system emergence and some data formats and operating systems may not be current. Consequently, many digital forensic tools demonstrate limited scope and require careful matching and mapping to the CI contexts to assure compatibility and effectiveness.

Importantly penetration tests are featured for the workstations and control rooms between the 'Search & Data Collection', and the 'Initial Assessment' phases. The penetration tests can confirm and limited the scope of further investigation. They can also provide vulnerability clues that redeploy of the 'Search & Data Collection' is done again for efficient targeting of areas for further investigation. This is a core component any CI forensic investigation. The major function of each one of these core components is to make sure that environments have correctly disclosed all the media for collection, and assurance is gained that complete analysis may proceed. The overall performance of an investigation will be limited unless the CI environmental and context variations can are fully addressed.

4.3 Big data investigation

The Hadoop context requires structured and planned entry for execution. The control for investigation comes from the central digital investigation phases and the management constraints. At any step acquired evidence can include different types of forensic data but the strategy is to organize the data into category and class nodes, and also data nodes. This organization and technical capability structures the data fields to optimize access at each phase of the central investigation plan. Live and dead nodes are discovered in a Hadoop architecture. They both contribute the necessary information needed to complete the digital forensic investigation on big data volumes. Nodes information is identified based on the different levels described in **Table 1**, such as node name with port number and IP address, last contact, admin state and additional information related to the data management and storage time and structure features. The scope includes all the logs created and stored on the cluster which contain the log files of data nodes, name nodes, secondary name nodes, the history server, user logs, the node manager, and the resource manager for all nodes. These files are vital for the process of hypotheses examination. To examine the Hadoop cluster, multimedia data acquisition techniques are used for the search and data collection. Data acquisition comes as a bit-by-bit copy of the content such as journal status, storage, log files, images, directories and logical database objects. The forensic examination is conducted through extracting system and nodes information using a range of proprietary and open source tools that are all selected and customized for the media type and performance. In this way the investigation phases can be executed in the big data context.

5. Penetration testing targeting

Cost efficiency is a critical factor in any digital investigation. Many elements, such as complexity and data volumes, hinder the efficient completion of investigation in CI environments. Consequently, strategies have to be employed to speed the completion without compromising the integrity of an investigation. Penetration testing is one such strategy. It is usually controlled and handled by penetration testers or qualified auditors and security specialists who are contracted in to scope the system and to identify useful investigation targets before the formal investigation proceeds. A penetration test seeks out the vulnerabilities of the system that an attacker could exploit, and where the system weaknesses are located. Such tests are performed from inside and outside the CI network infrastructure in order to test the overall performance of the network. The tests also determine the security level by categorizing the potential risks from high to low on the different interfaces. CI systems are a combination of applications interconnected to the control plane by network, hosts or branch networks. Penetration testing is a simulation process where real world attacks are made on potential targets to simulate the scope of hackers, attackers and other intruders. Penetration testing is also a valuable step towards developing a secure system that has assessed and mitigated potential vulnerabilities.

A basic penetration test may involve scanning for hosts' IP addresses in the network in order to check whether they are offering services with known vulnerabilities or hidden vulnerabilities that may be used in exploitation processes. The process would then extend to scanning ports for each host in the network and identifying unwanted opened ports that could be used as a gateway to the system. After following the penetration test plan the findings are reviewed and documented to be sent to stakeholders and investigators for action.

The objectives for penetration testing are [29, 30]:

- Preparing for the most effective starting test targets;
- Identification of security risks;
- Improving the performance of security systems;
- Prepare before an event occurs to prevent it; and,
- Reduce critical situations and potential crisis.

Important matters that come into consideration for planning CI penetration testing are aspects such as the scope, the intensity, the approach, the implementation techniques, and where to start. Each of these considerations will now be reviewed. The scope of the penetration test considers which systems and the degree to which each system will be tested. The cost may be reduced and complexity of the solution by limiting the extent of the testing in three categories:

- By performing Full penetration testing, the test will examine the overall performance and system safety policies of the target system.
- By performing Limited penetration testing, the access will include specific parts of the systems such as systems that are suspected hosts instead of testing the whole system.

- By performing Focused testing, where either one part of the system is tested or one service of the systems. The approach will provide only information about the test part not general information about the overall system security status.

The intensity of penetration testing is determined by the urgency of the situation. The urgency is measured by risk and is categorized into four metrics:

- Aggressive, is the highest level of penetration testing which generates a vast amount of network traffic about the infrastructure. The penetration tester tries to exploit all possible vulnerabilities in the system to identify whether the system is infected or secured. Some examples of aggressive attacks could be used in penetration testing such as Denial of Service attacks and buffer overflows. Calculated, cautious, and passive techniques are employed to get the best results. Covert and overt approaches are also used to sequence information gathering, and to achieve a comprehensive overview of a system. Different implementation techniques are also applied that differentiate characteristics of penetration tests and customize for the CI environment. The best approach, the motivation, and the important considerations when developing the optimal methodology and plan require sensitizing to the CI challenges. The implementation of an effective penetration testing plan can make an investigation cost efficient and deliver the best results earlier.

6. Conclusion

Conducting forensic investigations in industrial control systems is a complex process, not only because of the diversity of data and media, but also the variety of physical and logical partitions that are interconnected to the network including name nodes, data nodes and checkpoints. The research has delivered a framework for systematizing the process steps of investigation, and assuring the key issues of volume, format diversity, and management of data, are addressed. The innovation of featuring penetration testing into the investigation processes provides cost efficiencies and targeting towards completeness in an investigation. It steps beyond dependence on tool extraction of evidences, and justifies following the trail of evidence from the point(s) of greatest weakness and to the evidential media within the scope of a case. Such innovation improves assurance of completeness in an investigation and rigor for the methodologies. Digital forensic investigators are challenged by multimedia retrieval and data diversity. The proposed framework of methods is flexible and adaptable to multimedia environments, and assures control over the discovery processes.

Author details

Amr Adel[1*] and Brian Cusack[2]

1 Whitecliffe College of Technology and Innovation, Auckland, New Zealand

2 AUT University, Auckland, New Zealand

*Address all correspondence to: amra@whitecliffe.ac.nz

IntechOpen

References

[1] Phillips DM, Mazzuchi TA, Sarkani S. An architecture, system engineering, and acquisition approach for space system software resiliency. Information and Software Technology. 2018;**94**:150-164

[2] Khader M, Hadi A, Al-Naymat G. HDFS file operation fingerprints for forensic investigations. Digital Investigation. 2018;**24**:50-61

[3] Choure C, Patil LH. A Literature Survey on Intrusion Detection and Protection System using Data Mining. International Journal of Advance Research, Ideas and Innovations in Technology 2018;4:1.

[4] Regulation P. Regulation (EU) 2016/679 of the European Parliament and of the Council. REGULATION (EU). 2016;p.679.

[5] Qiu S, Liu J, Shi Y, Li M, Wang W. Identity-based private matching over outsourced encrypted datasets. IEEE Transactions on cloud Computing. 2015;23;6(3):747-59.

[6] Ahmad I, Abbas H, Raza A, Choo KK, Sajid A, Pasha M, Khan FA. Electronic crime investigations in a virtualised environment: a forensic process and prototype for evidence collection and analysis. Australian Journal of Forensic Sciences. 2018;4;50(2):183-208.

[7] Mouhtaropoulos A, Li CT, Grobler M. Digital forensic readiness: are we there yet. Journal International Computers, Law & Technology. 2014;**9**:173

[8] Jones J, Etzkorn L. Analysis of digital forensics live system acquisition methods to achieve optimal evidence preservation. IEEE SoutheastCon. 2016:1-6

[9] Shrivastava G, Kumar P, Gupta BB, Bala S, Dey N, editors. Handbook of Research on Network Forensics and Analysis Techniques. IGI Global; 2018

[10] Genge B, Graur F, Haller P. Experimental assessment of network design approaches for protecting industrial control systems. International Journal of Critical Infrastructure Protection. 2015;**11**:24-38

[11] Cherdantseva Y, Burnap P, Blyth A, Eden P, Jones K, Soulsby H, et al. A review of cyber security risk assessment methods for SCADA systems. Computers & security. 2016;**56**:1-27

[12] Stouffer K, Falco J, Scarfone K. Guide to industrial control systems (ICS) security. National Institute of Standards and Technology. 2008

[13] LeSaint J, Reed M, Popick P. System security engineering vulnerability assessments for mission-critical systems and functions. In: Proceedings of the Annual IEEE Systems Conference (SysCon). 13 Apr 2005. pp. 608-613

[14] Obregon L. Secure architecture for industrial control systems. SANS Institute InfoSec Reading Room. 2015 Sep.

[15] D'Orazio CJ, Choo KK. Circumventing iOS security mechanisms for APT forensic investigations: A security taxonomy for cloud apps. Future Generation Computer Systems. 2018;**79**:247-261

[16] Lutui R. A multidisciplinary digital forensic investigation process model. Business Horizons. 2016;**59**(6):593-604

[17] Adelstein F. Live forensics: diagnosing your system without killing it first. Communications of the ACM. 2006;**49**(2):63-66

[18] Martini B, Choo KK. Cloud forensic technical challenges and solutions: A snapshot. IEEE Cloud Computing. 2014;**1**(4):20-25

[19] Liu A, Fu H, Li Y. Secure and Trustworthy Forensic Data Acquisition and Transmission in a Cloud Infrastructure. World Scientific Book Chapters. 2018:167-191

[20] Qiu S, Liu J, Shi Y, Li M, Wang W. Identity-based private matching over outsourced encrypted datasets. IEEE Transactions on cloud Computing. 2015; 23;6(3):747-59.

[21] Awodele O, Onuiri EE, Okolie SO. Vulnerabilities in network infrastructures and prevention/ containment measures. In: Proceedings of Informing Science & IT Education Conference (InSITE) 2012.

[22] Broad J, Binder A. Hacking with kali, Practical Penetration Techniques. Waltham: Syngress; 2014

[23] Baloch R. Ethical hacking and penetration testing guide. Vol. 29. CRC Press; 2017

[24] Green J. Staying ahead of cyber-attacks. Network Security. 2015;1;(2):13-6.

[25] Singh S, Sharma PK, Moon SY, Moon D, Park JH. A comprehensive study on APT attacks and countermeasures for future networks and communications: challenges and solutions. The Journal of Supercomputing. 2019;**75**(8):4543-4574

[26] Northcutt S, Shenk J, Shackleford D, Rosenberg T, Siles R, Mancini S. Penetration testing: Assessing your overall security before attackers do. Sponsored by Core Impact, SANS Analyst Program 2006;3(6):22.

[27] Bradbury D. Point to own: the problem with hacking tools. Computer Fraud & Security. 2011;**2011**(11):12-14

[28] Yeo J. Using penetration testing to enhance your company's security. Computer Fraud & Security. 2013;**2013**(4):17-20

[29] Ficco M, Choraś M, Kozik R. Simulation platform for cyber-security and vulnerability analysis of critical infrastructures. Journal of computational science. 2017 Sep 1;**22**:179-186

[30] Sabillon R, Serra-Ruiz J, Cavaller V. An effective cybersecurity training model to support an organizational awareness program: The Cybersecurity Awareness TRAining Model (CATRAM). A Case Study in Canada. Journal of Cases on Information Technology (JCIT). 2019;21(3):26-39.

Section 4

Audio and Music Classification and Separation

Chapter 6

Classification and Separation of Audio and Music Signals

Abdullah I. Al-Shoshan

Abstract

This chapter addresses the topic of classification and separation of audio and music signals. It is a very important and a challenging research area. The importance of classification process of a stream of sounds come up for the sake of building two different libraries: speech library and music library. However, the separation process is needed sometimes in a cocktail-party problem to separate speech from music and remove the undesired one. In this chapter, some existed algorithms for the classification process and the separation process are presented and discussed thoroughly. The classification algorithms will be divided into three categories. The first category includes most of the real time approaches. The second category includes most of the frequency domain approaches. However, the third category introduces some of the approaches in the time-frequency distribution. The approaches of time domain discussed in this chapter are the short-time energy (STE), the zero-crossing rate (ZCR), modified version of the ZCR and the STE with positive derivative, the neural networks, and the roll-off variance. The approaches of the frequency spectrum are specifically the roll-off of the spectrum, the spectral centroid and the variance of the spectral centroid, the spectral flux and the variance of the spectral flux, the cepstral residual, and the delta pitch. The time-frequency domain approaches have not been yet tested thoroughly in the process of classification and separation of audio and music signals. Therefore, the spectrogram and the evolutionary spectrum will be introduced and discussed. In addition, some algorithms for separation and segregation of music and audio signals, like the independent Component Analysis, the pitch cancelation and the artificial neural networks will be introduced.

Keywords: audio signal, music signal, classification, separation, time domain, frequency domain, time-frequency domain

1. Introduction

Audio signal processing is an important subfield of signal processing that is concerned with the electronic manipulation of audio signals [1–6]. The problem of discriminating music from audio has increasingly become very important as automatic audio signal recognition (ASR) systems and it has been increasingly applied in the domain of real-world multimedia [7]. Human's ear can easily distinguish audio without any influence of the mixed music [8–23]. Due to the new methods of the analysis and the synthesis processing of audio signals, the processing of musical signals has gained particular weight [16, 24], and therefore, the classical sound analysis methods may be used in the processing of musical signals [25–28]. Many types of musical signals such as Rock music, Pop music, Classical music, Country music, Latin music, Arabic music, Disco and Jazz, Electronic music, etc. are existed [29]. The sound type signals hierarchy is shown in **Figure 1** [30].

Audio signal changes randomly and continuously through time. As an example, music and audio signals have strong energy content in the low frequencies and weaker energy content in the high frequencies [31, 32]. **Figure 2** depicts a generalized time and frequency spectra of audio signals [33]. The maximum frequency f_{max} varies according to type of audio signal, where, in the telephone transmission f_{max} is equal to 4 kHz, 5 kHz in mono-loudspeaker recording, 6 KHz in multi-loudspeaker recording or stereo, 11 kHz in FM broadcasting, however, it equals to 22 KHz in the CD recording.

Acoustically speaking, the audio signals can be classified into the following classes:

1. Single talker in specific time [34].

2. Singing without music.

3. Mixture of background music and single talker audio.

4. Songs that are a mixture of music with a singer voice.

5. May completely be music signal without any audio component.

6. Complex sound mixture like multi-singers or multi-speakers with multi-music sources.

Figure 1.
Types of audio signals.

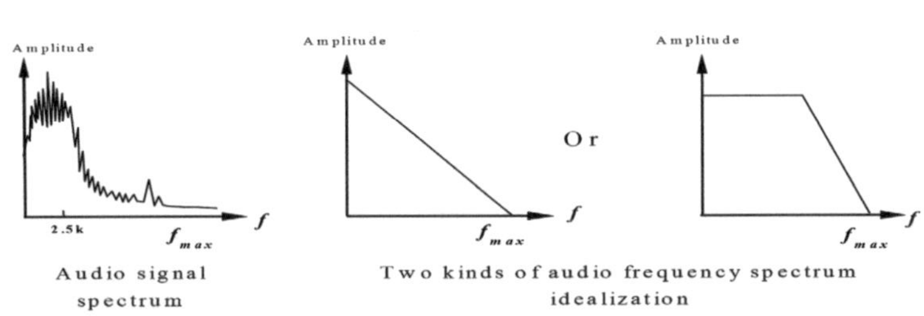

Figure 2.
Generalized frequency spectrum for audio signal [33].

7. Non-music and non-audio signals: like fan, motor, car, jet sounds, etc.

8. Audio signal that is a mixture of more than one speakers talking simultaneously at the same time [8].

9. Abnormal music can be single word cadence, human whistle sound, or opposite reverberation [4, 34–38].

2. Analysis of audio and music signals

2.1 Properties of audio signal

2.1.1 Representation of audio signal

The letters symbols used for writing are not adequate, as the way they are pronounced varies; for example, the letter "o" in English, is pronounced differently in words "pot" most" and "one". It is almost impossible to tackle the audio classification problem without first establishing some way of representing the spoken utterances by some group of symbols representing the sounds produced [39–43]. The phonemes in **Table 1** are divided into groups based on the way they are produced [44], forming a set of *allophones* [45]. In some tonal languages, such as Vietnamese and Mandarin, the intonation determines the meaning of each word [46–48].

2.1.2 Production of audio signal

Since the range of sounds that can be produced by any system is limited [39–44], the pressure in the lungs is increased by the reverse process. They push the air up the *trachea*; the larynx is situated at the top of the trachea. By changing the shape of the vocal tract, different sounds are produced, so the fundamental frequency will be changing with time. The spectrogram (or sonogram) for the sentence "What can I have for dinner tonight?" is shown in **Figure 3**.

Vowels	Diphthongs	Fricatives	Plosives	Semivowels	Nasals	Affricates
heed	bay	sail	bat	was	am	jaw
hid	by	ship	disc	ran	an	chore
head	bow	funnel	Goat	lot	sang	
had	bough	thick	pool	yacht		
hard	beer	hull	tap			
hod	doer	zoo	kite			
hoard	boar	azure				
hood	boy	that				
who'd	bear	valve				
hut						
heard						
the						

Table 1.
Phoneme categories of British English and examples of words in which they are used [44].

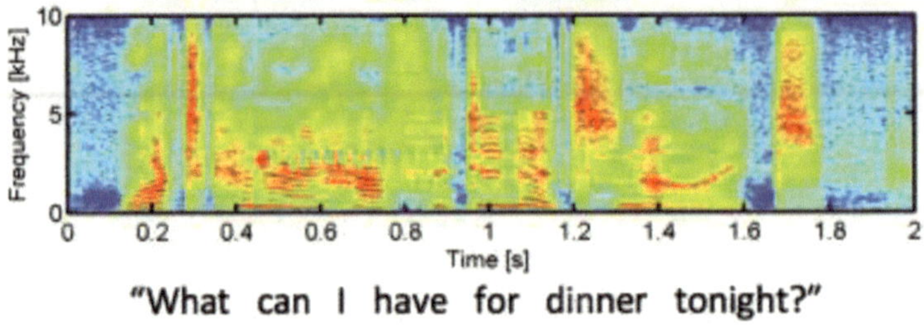

Figure 3.
A sonogram for the sentence "What can I have for dinner tonight?" [43].

The way that humans recognize and interpret audio signal has been considered by many researchers [1, 25, 39]. To produce a complete set of English vowels, many researchers have depicted that the two lowest formants are necessary, as well as that the three lowest formants in frequency are necessary for good audio intelligibility. As the number of formants increased, sounds that are more natural are produced. However, when we deal with continues audio, the problem becomes more complex. The history of audio signal identification can be found in [1, 25, 39–48].

2.2 Properties of music signal

2.2.1 Representation of music signal

There are two kinds of tone structures in music signal. The first one is a simple tone formed of single sinusoidal waveform, however, the second one is a more complex tone consisting of more than one harmonic [31, 49–52]. The spectrum of music signal has twice the bandwidth of audio spectrum, and most of the power of audio signal is concentrated at lower frequencies. Melodists and musicians divide musical minor to eight parts and each part named octave, where each octave is divided into seven parts called tones [30]. For different instrument, a tempered scale is shown in **Table 2**. These tones, shown in **Table 2**, are named (Do, Re, Me, Fa, So, La and Se) or simply (A, B, C, D, E, F, and G). The tone (A1) at the first octave has the fundamental frequency of the first tone in each octave, i.e., every first tone in each octave takes the reduplicate frequency of the first tone of previous one, (i.e., $An = 2^n A1$ or $Bn = 2^n B1$ and so on where $n \in \{2, 3, 4, 5, 6, 7\}$.

From **Table 2**, the highest tone C8 occurs at the frequency of 4186 Hz, which is the highest frequency produced by human sound system, which leads musical

A Hz	B Hz	C Hz	D Hz	E Hz	F Hz	G Hz
A_1 27.5	B_1 30.863	C_1 32.703	D_1 36.708	E_1 41.203	F_1 43.654	G_1 48.99
A_2 55	B_2 61.735	C_2 65.406	D_2 73.416	E_2 82.407	F_2 87.307	G_2 97.99
A_3 110	B_3 123.47	C_3 130.81	D_3 146.83	E_3 164.81	F_3 174.61	G_3 196
A_4 220	B_4 246.94	C_4 261.63	D_4 293.66	E_4 329.63	F_4 349.23	G_4 392
A_5 440	B_5 493.88	C_5 523.25	D_5 587.33	E_5 659.26	F_5 698.46	G_5 783.9
A_6 880	B_6 987.77	C_6 1046.5	D_6 1174.7	E_6 1318.5	F_6 1396.9	G_6 1568
A_7 176	B_7 1975.5	C_7 2093	D_7 2349.3	E_7 2637	F_7 2793	G_7 3136
A_8 352	B_8 3951.1	C_8 4186				

Table 2.
Frequencies of notes in the tempered scale [3].

instrument manufactures to try their best to bound music frequency to human's sound system limits to achieve strong concord [35, 53, 54]. In the real world, musical instruments cover more frequencies than audible band, which is limited to 20 kHz).

2.2.2 Production of music signal

The concept of tone quality that is most common depends on the subjective acoustic properties, regardless of partials or formants and the production of music depends mainly on the kind of musical instruments [53, 54]. These instruments can be summarized as follows:

1. **The string musical instrument.** Its tones is produced by vibrating chords made from horsetail hair, or other manufactured material like copper or plastic. Every vibrating chord has its own fundamental frequency, producing complex tones so that it covers most of the audible bands. **Figure 4** shows string instruments.

2. **The brass musical instrument.** The Brass musical instrument depends on blowing air like woodwind. Its shape looks like an animal horn and has manual valves to control cavity size. Brass musical instrument has huge number of nonharmonic signals existed in its spectrum. **Figure 5** shows brass instruments.

3. **The woodwind musical instrument.** Woodwind instrument consists of an open cylindrical tube at both ends. Some woodwind instruments may use small-vibrated piece of copper to produce tones. It produces many numbers of harmonic tones. **Figure 6** shows woodwind instruments.

4. **The percussion musical instrument.** Examples of percussion instruments are piano, snare drum, chimes, marimba, timpani, and xylophone. Most of the power of tones in percussion instruments produces non-harmonic components. **Figure** 7 shows some percussion instruments.

5. **The electronic musical instrument.** The most qualified robust and accurate electronic musical instrument is the organ. It has a large keyboard, a memory that can store notes and use their frequencies as basic cadences or tones. Without organ help, disco, pop, rock and jazz cannot stand [29, 35–38]. Organ is not the only electronic musical producer. If the electronic musical

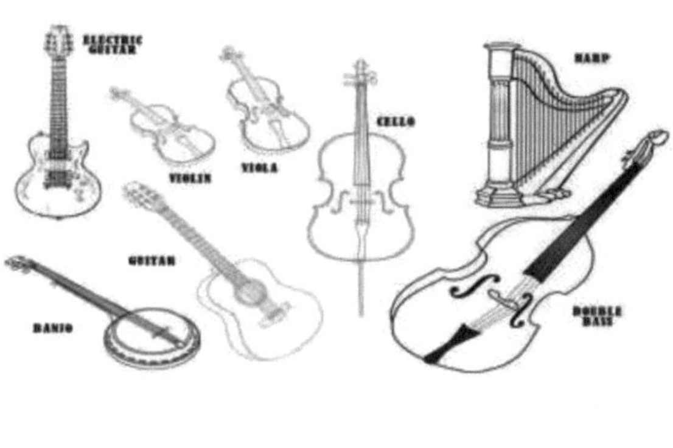

Figure 4.
String instruments.

Figure 5.
Brass instruments.

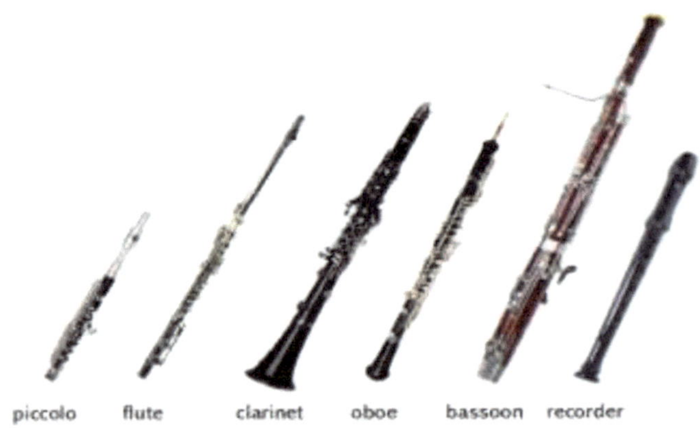

Figure 6.
Woodwind instruments.

instruments are used for producing music, the tone quality measure of the fundamental frequency or harmonics is not needed. **Figure 8** shows an example of organ electronic instrument.

2.3 Characteristics and differences between audio and music

The audio signal is a slowly time varying signal in the sense that, when examined over a sufficiently short period of time "between 5 and 100 *msec*. Therefore, its characteristics are stationary within this period of time. A simple example of an audio signal is shown in **Figure 9**.

Figure 10 is a typical example of music portion. It is very clear from the two spectrums in **Figures 9** and **10** that we can distinguish between the two types of signals.

Figures 11 and **12** depict the evolutionary spectrum of two different types of signals, audio and music.

Now, let us discuss some of the main similarity and differences between the two types of signals.

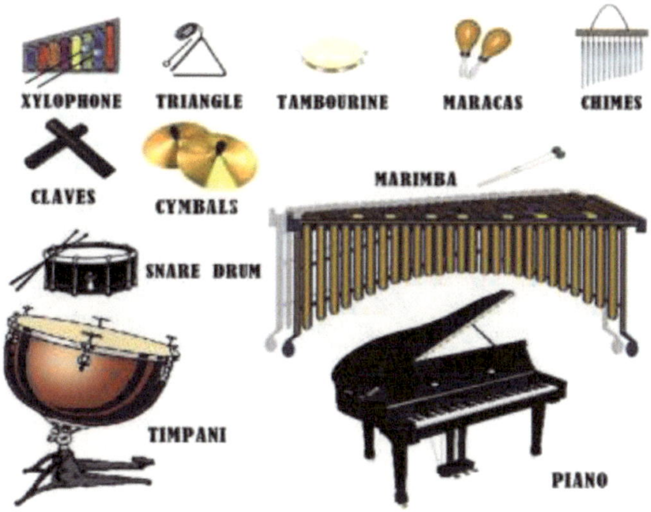

Figure 7.
Percussion instruments.

Figure 8.
Electronic organ.

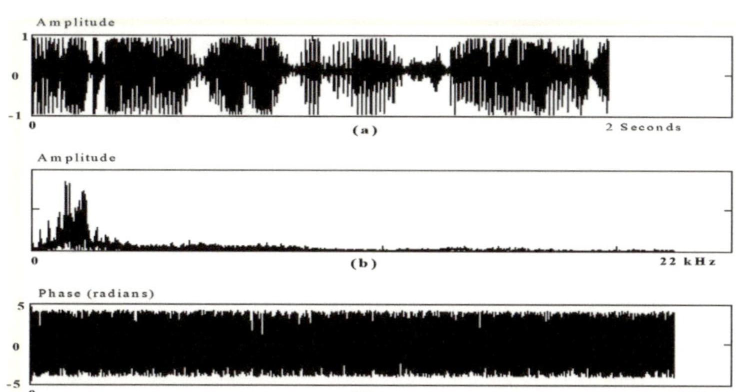

Figure 9.
An example of audio signal of specking the two-second long phrase "Very good night"*: (a) time domain (b) magnitude. (c) Phase.*

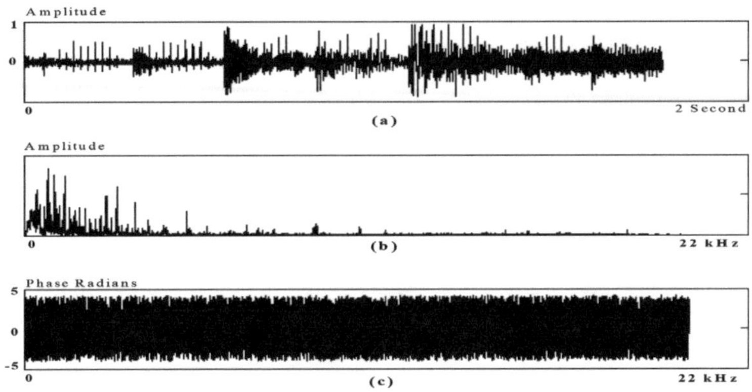

Figure 10.
A 2-second long music signal: (a) time domain. (b) Spectrum. (c) Phase.

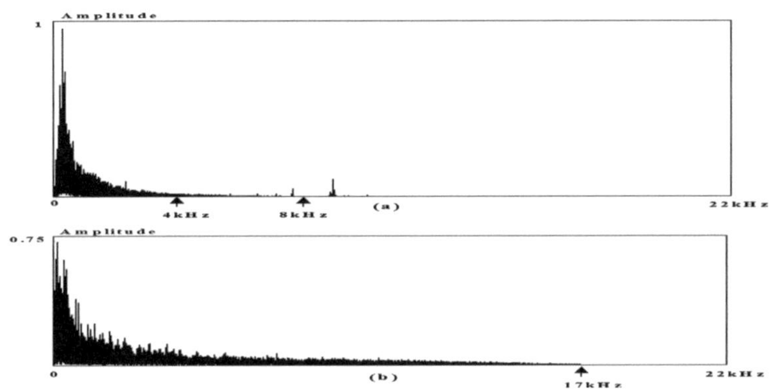

Figure 11.
The spectrum of an average of 500 specimens: (a) audio, (b) music.

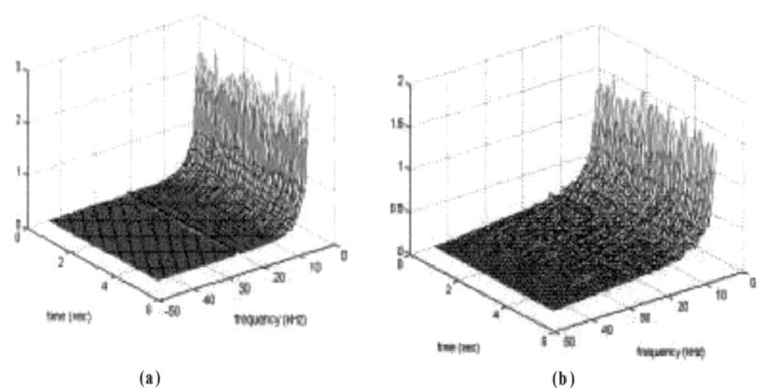

Figure 12.
Evolutionary spectrum of an average of 500 specimens: (a) audio, (b) music.

Tonality. By tone, we mean a single harmonic of a pure periodical sinusoid. Regardless of the type of instruments or music, the musical signal is composed of a multiple of tones; however, this is not the case in the voice signal [47, 52, 55–57].

Bandwidth. Normally, the audio signal has 90% of its power concentrated within frequencies lower than 4 kHz and limited to 8 kHz; however, music signal can extend its power to the upper limits of the ear's response, which is 20 kHz [52, 58].

Alternative sequence. Audio exhibits an alternating sequence of noise-like segment while music alternates in more tonal shape. In other words, audio signal is distributed through its spectrum more randomly than music does.

Power distribution. Normally, the power distribution of an audio signal is concentrated at frequencies lower than 4 kHz, and then collapsed rapidly above this frequency. On the other hand, there is no specific shape of the power of music spectrum [59].

Dominant frequency. For a single talker, his dominant frequency can accurately be determined uniquely, however, in a single musical instrument only the average dominant frequency can be determined. In multiple musical instruments, the case will be worst.

Fundamental frequency. For a single talker, his fundamental frequency can be accurately configured. However, this is not the case for a single music instrument.

Excitation patterns. The excitation signals (pitch) for audio are usually existed only over a span of three octaves, while the fundamental music tones can span up to six octaves [60].

Energy sequences. A reasonable generalization is that audio follows a pattern of high-energy conditions of voicing followed by low energy conditions, which the envelope of music is less likely to exhibit.

Tonal duration. The duration of vowels in audio is very regular, following the syllabic rate. Music exhibits a wider variation in tone lengths, not being constrained by the process of articulation. Hence, tonal duration would likely be a good discriminator.

Consonants. Audio signal contains too many consonants while music is usually continuous through the time [33].

Zero crossing rate (ZCR). The ZCR in music is greater than that in audio. We can use this idea to design a discriminator [60].

In the frequency domain, there is a strong overlapping between audio and music signals, so no ordinary filter can separate them. As mentioned before, audio signal may cover spectrum between 0 and 4 kHz with a dominant frequency of an average = 1.8747 kHz. However, the lowest fundamental frequency (A1) of a music signal is about 27.5 Hz and the highest frequency of the tone C8 is around 4186 Hz. The reason behind this is that musical instrument manufacturers try to bound music frequency to human's sound limits in order to achieve a strong consonant and a strong frequency overlap. Moreover, music may propagate over the audible

Key Difference	Audio	Music
Units of Analysis	**Phonemes**	**Notes Finite**
Temporal Structure	• Short sample (40 ms–200 ms). • More steady state than dynamic. • Timing unstrained but variable. • Amplitude modulation rate for sentences is slow (~ 4 Hz)	• Longer sample: 600–1200 ms. • Mix of steady state (strings, winds) and transient (percussion). • Strong periodicity.
Spectral Structure	• Largely harmonic (vowels, voiced consonants). • Tend to group in formants. • Some inharmonic stops.	• Largely harmonic and some inharmonic (percussion).
Syntactic / Semantic Structure	• Symbolic • Productive • Can be combined in grammar	• Symbolic • Productive • Combined in a grammar

Table 3.
The main differences between audio and music signals.

spectrum to cover more than the audible band of 20 kHz, with a dominant frequency of an average = 1.9271 kHz [25].

Table 3 summarizes the main similarity and differences between music and audio signals.

3. Audio and music signals classification

The main classification approaches will be discussed in this section. They can be categorized into three different approaches: (1) time domain approaches, (2) frequency domain approaches, and (3) time-frequency domain approaches. A two-level music and audio classifier was developed by El-Maleh [61, 62]. He used a combination of long-term features such as the variance, the differential parameters, the zero crossing rate (ZCR), and the time-averages of spectral parameters. Saunders [60] proposed another two-level classifier. His approach was based on the short-time energy (STE) and the average ZCR features. In addition, Matityaho and Furst [63] have developed a neural network based model for classifying music signals. Their model was designed based on human cochlea functional performance.

For audio detection, Hoyt and Wecheler [64] have developed a neural network base model using Fourier transform, Hamming filtering, and a logarithmic function as pre-processing then they applied a simple threshold algorithm for detecting audio, music, wind, traffic or any interfering sound. In addition, to improve the performance, they suggested wavelet transform feature for pre-processing. Their work is much similar to the work done by Matityaho and Furst's [63, 64]. 13 features were examined by Scheirer and Slaney [65]. Some of these features were simple modification of each other's. They also tried combining them in several multidimensional classification forms. From these previous works, the most powerful discrimination features were the STE and the ZCR. Therefore, the STE and the ZCR will be discussed thoroughly. Finally, the common classifiers of the audio and the music signals can be divided into the following approaches:

I. **The Time domain algorithms**:

1. The ZCR algorithm [1, 34, 66–77]:

    a. The standard deviation of first order difference of the ZCR.

    b. The 3rd central moment of the mean of ZCR.

    c. The total number of zero crossings exceeding a specific threshold.

2. The STE [60–65, 78].

3. The ZCR and the STE positive derivative [78, 79].

4. The Pulse Metric [31, 59, 80–82].

5. The number of silence [32, 60].

6. The HMM (Hidden Markov Model) [83–85].

7. The ANN (Artificial neural networks) [12, 49, 58, 63, 79, 83–120].

8. The Roll-Off Variance [31, 59].

II. **The Frequency-domain algorithms** [32, 33, 35, 59, 112, 66–77, 121]:

1. The Spectrum [31, 111]:

    a. The Spectral Centroid.

    b. The Spectral Flux Variance.

    c. The Spectral Centroid Mean and Variance.

    d. The Spectral Flux Mean and Variance.

    e. The Spectrum Roll-Off.

    f. The Signal Bandwidth.

    g. The Spectrum Amplitude.

    h. The Delta Amplitude.

2. The Cepstrum [122]:

    a. The Cepstral Residual [122–124].

    b. The Variance of the Cepstral Residual [122–124].

    c. The Cepstral feature [122–124].

    d. The Pitch [94, 107, 108, 117–119, 125, 126].

    e. The Delta Pitch [88, 119].

III. **The Time-Frequency domain algorithms**:

1. The Spectrogram (or Sonogram) [13, 19, 86, 127].

2. The Evolutionary Spectrum and the Evolutionary Bispectrum [81, 128, 129].

3.1 Time domain algorithms

3.1.1 The ZCR algorithm

The ZCR algorithm can be defined as the number of crossing the signal the zero axis within a specific window. It is widely used because its simplicity and robustness [34]. We may define the ZCR as in the following equation.

$$Z_n = \frac{1}{2N} \sum_{m=n-N+1}^{N} | \, sgn\,[x(m)] - sgn\,[x(m-1)]| \tag{1}$$

where Z_n is the ZCR, N is the number of samples in one window, and sgn is the sign of the signal such that $sgn\,[x(n)] = 1$ when $x(n) > 0$, $sgn\,[x(n)] = -1$, when $x(n) < 0$. An essential not is that the sampling rate must be high enough to catch any crossing through zero. Another important note before evaluating the ZCR is to normalize the signal by subtracting its average value. It is clear from Eq. (1) that the value of the ZCR is proportional to the sign change in the signal, i.e., the dominant frequency of $x(n)$. Therefore, we may find that the ZCR of music is, in general, higher than that of audio, but not sure at the unvoiced audio.

Properties of ZCR:

The ZCR properties can be summarized as follow.

1. **The Principle of Dominant Frequency**

The dominant frequency of a pure sinusoid is the only value in the spectrum. This value of frequency is equal to the ZCR of the signal in one period. If we have a non-sinusoidal periodic signal, its dominant frequency is frequency with the largest amplitude. The dominant frequency (ω_0) can be evaluated as follow.

$$\omega_o = \frac{\pi E\{D_o\}}{N-1} \quad (2)$$

where N is the number of intervals, $E\{.\}$ is the expected value, and D_o is the ZCR per interval.

2. **The Highest frequency**

Since D_0 denotes the ZCR of a discrete-time signal $Z(i)$, let us assume that D_n denotes the ZCR of the nth derivative of $Z(i)$, i.e., D_1 is the ZCR of the first derivative of $Z(i)$, D_2 is the ZCR of the second derivative of $Z(i)$, and so on. Then, the highest frequency ω_{max} in the signal can be evaluated as follow.

$$\omega_{max} = \lim_{i\to\infty} \frac{\pi\, E\{D_i\}}{N-1} \quad (3)$$

where N is the number of samples. If the sampling rate equals 11 KHz, then the change in ω_{max} can be ignored for $i > 10$.

3. **The Lowest frequency**

Assuming that the time period between any two samples is normalized to unity, the derivative of $Z(i)$ can be defined as $Z(i) = Z(i) - Z(i{-}1)$. Then, the ZCR of the nth derivative of $Z(i)$ is defined as D_n. Now, let us define ∇^+ as the +ve derivative of $Z(i)$, then $\nabla^+ [Z(i)]$ can be defined as follow.

$$\nabla^+[Z(i)] = Z(i) + Z(i-1) \quad (4)$$

Now, let us define the ZCR of the nth + ve derivative of $Z(i)$ by the symbol ${}_nD$. Then we can find the lowest frequency ω_{min} of a signal as follow.

$$W_{min} = \lim_{i\to\infty} \frac{\pi\, E\{{}_iD\}}{N-1} \quad (5)$$

4. **Measure of Periodicity**

   A signal is said to be purely periodic if and only if.

$$E\{{}_1D\} = E\{{}_2D\} \tag{6}$$

   Using Eq. (6), it was found that music is more periodic or than audio [44–47, 55–57, 130].

The Ratio of High ZCR (RHZCR)

It was found that the variation of the ZCR is more discriminative than the exact ZCR, so the RHZCR can be considered as one feature [78]. The RHZCR is defined as the ratio of the number of frames whose ZCR are above 1 over the average ZCR in one-window, and can be defined as follow.

$$\text{RHZCR} = \frac{1}{2N} \sum_{n=0}^{N-1} [\,\text{sgn}\,(\text{ZCR}(n) - \text{ZCR}_{av}) + 1 \tag{7}$$

$$\text{ZCR}_{av} = \sum_{n=0}^{N-1} \text{ZCR}(n) \tag{8}$$

where N is the number of frames per one-window, n is the index of the frame, sgn[.] is a sign function and ZCR(n) is the zero-crossing rate at the nth frame. In general, audio signals consist of alternating voiced and unvoiced sounds in each syllable rate, while music does not have this kind of alternation. Therefore, from Eq. (7) and Eq. (8), we may observe that the variation of the ZCR (or the RHZCR) in an audio signal is greater than that of a music, as shown in **Figure 13**.

3.1.2 The STE algorithm

The amplitude of the audio signal varies appreciably with time. In particular, the amplitude of unvoiced segments is generally much lower than the amplitude of voiced segments. The STE of the audio signal provides a convenient representation

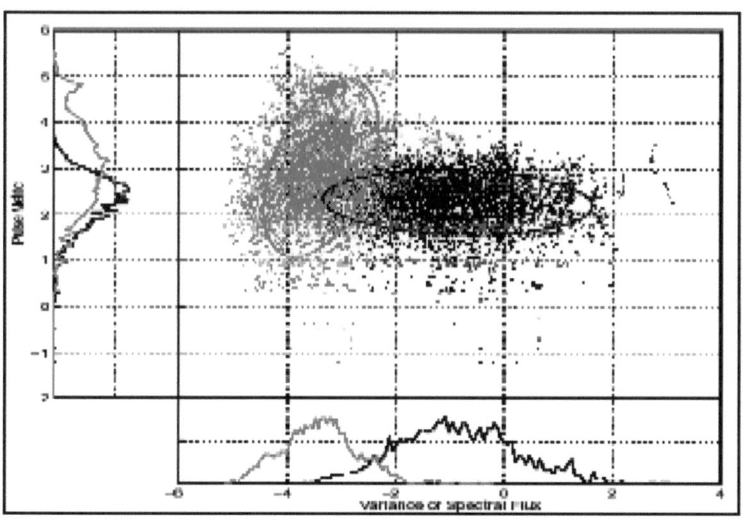

Figure 13.
Music and audio sharing some values [65].

that reflects these amplitude variations. Unlike the audio signal, since the music signal does not contain unvoiced segments, the STE of the music signal is usually bigger than that of audio [60]. The STE of a discrete-time signal $s(n)$ can define as.

$$\mathrm{STE_S} = \sum_{n=-\infty}^{\infty} |s(n)|^2 \tag{9}$$

where $\mathrm{STE_s}$ in Eq. (9) is the total energy of the signal. The average power of $s(n)$ is defined as.

$$P_s = \lim_{N\to\infty} \frac{1}{2N+1} \sum_{n=-N}^{N} |s(n)^2| \tag{10}$$

Signals can be classified into three types, in general: an energy signal, which has a non-zero and finite energy, a power signal, which has a non-zero and finite energy, and the third type is neither energy nor power signal, see **Table 4**. Now, let us define another sequence $\{f(n;m)\}$ as follow.

$$f_s(n, m) = s(n)w(m-n) \tag{11}$$

where $w(n)$ is just a window with a length of N with a value of zero outside $[0, N\text{-}1]$. Therefore, $f_s(n,m)$ will be zero outside $[m\text{-}N + 1, m]$.

Deriving short term features

The silence and unvoiced period in audios can be considered a stochastic background noise. Now, let us define F_s as a feature of $\{s(n)\}$, mapping its values of the Hilbert space, H, to a set of complex numbers C such that.

$$F_s : H \to C \tag{12}$$

The long-term feature of $\{s(n)\}$ may be defined as follow.

$$L\{s(n)\} = \lim_{N\to\infty} \frac{1}{2N+1} \sum_{n=-N}^{N} s(n) \tag{13}$$

The long-term average, when applied to energy signals, will have zero values, however, it is appropriate for power signals. Eq. (13) can be re-written as follow.

$$L\{s(n)\} = \frac{1}{2N} \sum_{n=-\infty}^{\infty} s(n) \tag{14}$$

Energy Signal $0 < E_s < \infty$	Transient	$S(n) = \alpha^n u(n)\ \lvert\alpha\rvert < 1$
	Finite Sequence	$e^{\beta t}[u(n)\text{-}u(n\text{-}255)]\ \lvert\beta\rvert < \infty$
Power Signal $0 < P_s < \infty$	Constant	$s(n) = \alpha\ \text{-}\infty < \alpha < \infty$
	Periodic	$s(n) = \alpha \sin(n\omega_o + \varphi)\ \text{-}\infty < \alpha < \infty$
	Stochastic	$S(n)$ = rand (seed)
Neither Energy nor Power Signal	Zero	$s(n) = 0$
	Blow up	$s(n) = \alpha^n u(n)\ \lvert\alpha\rvert > 1$

Table 4.
Types of signals.

Resulting a family of mappings. If each member of the family is selected to be a λ, the we can use the notation $F_s(\lambda)$. The discrete-time Fourier transforms is an example of a parametric long-term feature. The long-term feature can be of the form.

$$L\{M(\lambda)\{s(n)\}\} \tag{15}$$

where M in Eq. (15) is the mapping sequence. It maps $\{s(n)\}$ to another sequence. The long-term feature $F_s(\lambda)$ is defined as $L^o M$, a composition of function L and M. If $F_s(\lambda)$ is the long-term feature of Eq. (12), then the short-term feature $F_s(\lambda, m)$ of time period m can be constructed as follows:

- Define a frame as in Eq. (11).
- Apply the long-term feature transformation to the frame sequence as in Eq. (16).

$$\begin{aligned} F_s(\lambda, m) &= L\{M(\lambda)\}\{f_s(n, m)\} \\ &= L\{M(\lambda)\}\{s(n)w(m-n)\} \\ &= \frac{1}{N}\sum_{n=-\infty}^{\infty} M(\lambda)\{s(n)w(m-n)\} \end{aligned} \tag{16}$$

Low Short Time Energy Ratio (LSTER)

As done in the ZCR, the variation is selected [33]. Here, the LSTER is used to represent the variation of the STE. LSTER is defined as the ratio of the number of frames whose STE are less than 0.5 times of the average STE in a one-second window, as in Eq. (17).

$$\text{LSTER} = \frac{1}{2N}\sum_{n=0}^{N-1}[\text{sgn}\,(0.5\text{STE}_{av} - \text{STE}(n) + 1] \tag{17}$$

where.

$$\text{STE}_{av} = \sum_{n=0}^{N-1} \text{STE}(n) \tag{18}$$

N is the total number of frames, $\text{STE}(n)$ is the STE at the nth frame, and STE_{av} in Eq. (18) is the average STE in a one-window.

3.1.3 The effect of positive derivation

Figure 14 shows the preprocessing flow on $Z(i)$ using the positive derivation concept (+), which provided some improvement in the discrimination process [78].

This pre-processing increased the ZCR of music and reduced the ZCR of the audio with the expenses of some delay. The averages of the ZCR in speech, mixture, and music are shown in **Figure 15**, after applying the +ve derivative of order 50.

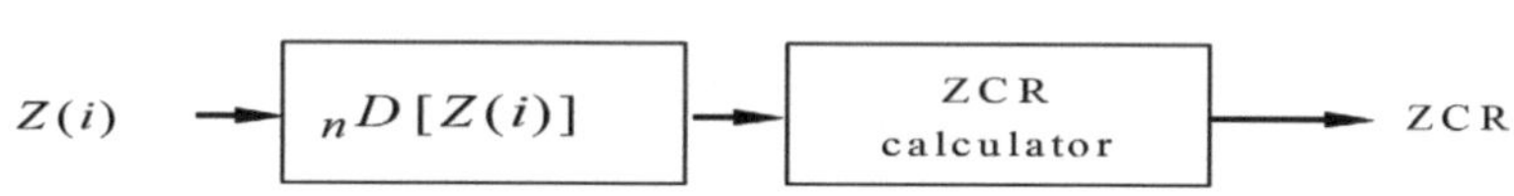

Figure 14.
The preprocessing using the +ve derivative before evaluating the ZCR.

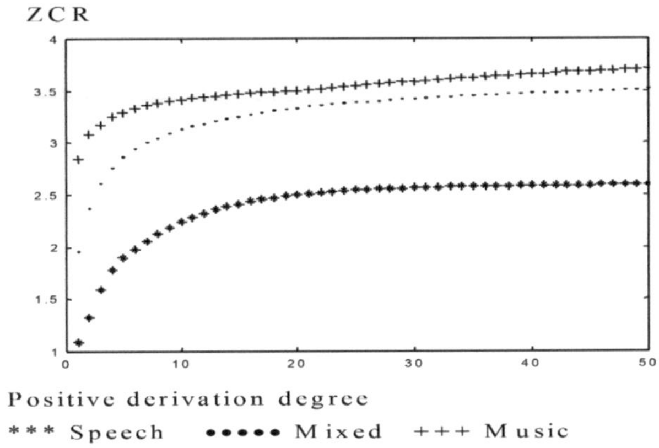

Figure 15.
The average ZCR of speech, mixture, and music, after pre-processing with the +ve derivative [78].

3.1.4 Artificial neural network (ANN) approach

The ANN approach is a multipurpose technique that was used for implementing many algorithms [14, 36, 63, 79, 86–105, 110, 125], especially in classification issues [16, 49, 107–111, 119, 120, 131, 132]. A multi-layer ANN approach was used in many classification tools since it can represent nonlinear decision support systems.

3.2 Algorithms in the frequency domain

3.2.1 The spectrum approaches

3.2.1.1 Spectral flux mean and variance

This feature characterizes the change in the shape of the spectrum so it measures frame-to-frame spectral difference. Audio signals go through less frame-to-frame changes than music. The spectral flux values in audio signal is lower than that of music.

The spectral flux, sometimes called the *delta spectrum magnitude*, is defined as the *second norm* of the spectral amplitude of the difference vector and defined as in Eq. (19).

$$\mathrm{SF} = \| \; |X(k)\text{-}|X(k+1)| \, | \; \| \tag{19}$$

where $X(k)$ is the signal power and k is the corresponding frequency. Another definition of the SF is also described as follow.

$$\mathrm{SF} = \frac{1}{(N-1)(M-1)} \sum_{n=1}^{N-1} \sum_{k=1}^{M-1} [\; \log\; (A(n,k)+\delta) - \log\; (A(n-1,k)+\delta)]^2 \tag{20}$$

where $A(n,k)$ in Eq. (20) is the discrete Fourier transform (DFT) of the nth frame of the input signal and can be described as in Eq. (21).

$$A(n,k) = \left| \sum_{m=-\infty}^{\infty} x(m) w(nL-m) e^{j\frac{2\pi}{L}km} \right| \tag{21}$$

and $x(m)$ is the original audio data, L is the window length, M is the order of the DFT, N is the total number of frames, δ is an arbitrary constant, and $w(m)$ is the

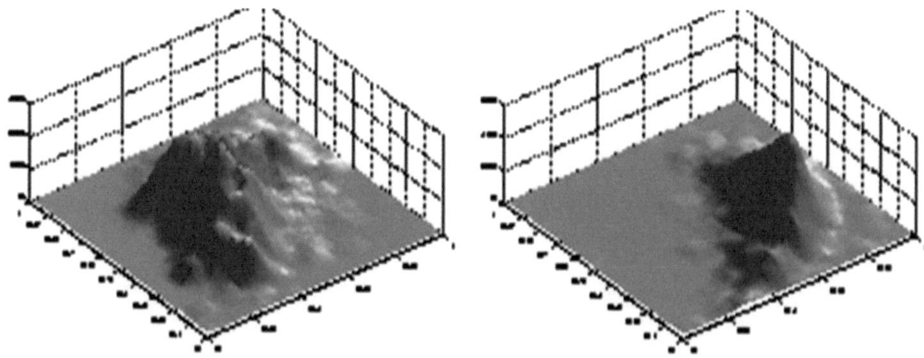

(a) (b)

Figure 16.
3D histogram normalized features (the mean and the variance of spectral flux) of: (a) music signal, (b) audio signal [133].

	Training	Testing	Cross-validation
GMM	8.0%	8.1%	8.2%
kNN	X	6.0%	8.9%
ANN	6.7%	6.9%	11.6%

Table 5.
Percentage of misclassified segments [133].

window function. Scheirer and Slaney [65] has found that *SF* feature is very useful in discriminating audio from music. **Figure 16** depicts that the variances are lower for music than for audio, and the means are less for audio than for music signal. Rossignol and others [133] have computed the means and variances of a one-second segment using frames of length 18 milliseconds.

Rossignol and others [133] have tested three classification approaches to classify the segments. They used the k-nearest-neighbors (kNN) with k = seven, the Gaussian mixture model (GMM), and the ANN classifiers. **Table 5** shows their results are shown in **Table 5**, using the mean and the variance of the SF.

3.2.1.2 The mean and variance of the spectral centroid

In the frequency domain, the mean and variance of the spectral centroid feature describes the center of frequency at which most of the power in the signal is found. In audio signals, the pitches of the signals are concentrated in narrow range of low frequencies. In contrast, music signals have higher frequencies that result higher spectral means, i.e., higher spectral centroids. For a frame at time t, the spectral centroid can be evaluated as follows.

$$\mathrm{SC} = \frac{\sum_k kX(k)}{\sum_k X(k)} \tag{22}$$

where $X(k)$ is the power of the signal at the corresponding frequency band k. When the mean and the variance of the SP are combined with the mean and the variance of the SC in Eq. (22), and the mean and the variance of the ZCR, the results of **Table 6** are found.

	Training	Testing	Cross-validation
GMM	7.9%	7.3%	22.9%
kNN	X	2.2%	5.8%
ANN	4.7%	4.6%	9.1%

Table 6.
Percentage of misclassified segments [133].

3.2.1.3 Energy at 4 Hz modulation

Audio signal has an energy peak centered on the 4 Hz syllabic rate. Therefore, a 2nd order band pass filter is used, with center frequency of 4 Hz. Although audio signals have higher energy at that 4 Hz, some music bass instruments was found to have modulation energy around this frequency [65, 133].

3.2.1.4 Roll-off point

In the frequency domain, the roll-off point feature is the value of the frequency that has 95% of the power of the signal. The value of the roll-off point can be found as follow [65, 133].

$$\sum_{k<v} X(k) = (0.95)\sum_{k} X(k) \tag{23}$$

where the left hand side of Eq. (23) is the sum of the power at the frequency value V, and the right hand side of Eq. (23) is the 95% of the total power of the signal of the frame, and $X(k)$ is the DFT of $x(t)$.

3.2.2 Cepstrum

The cepstrum of a signal can be defined as the inverse of the DFT of the logarithm of the spectrum of a signal. Music signals have higher cepstrum values than that of speech ones. The complex cepstrum is defined in the following Equation [122–124].

$$\hat{X}\left(e^{j\omega}\right) = \log\left[X\left(e^{j\omega}\right)\right] = \log\left|X\left(e^{j\omega}\right)\right| + j\arg\left[X\left(e^{j\omega}\right)\right] \tag{24}$$

and then.

$$\hat{x}(n) = \frac{1}{2\pi}\int_{-\pi}^{\pi} \hat{X}\left(e^{j\omega n}\right) d\omega \tag{25}$$

where $X(e^{j\omega})$ is the DFT of the sequence $x(n)$.

3.2.3 Summary

Table 7 summarizes the percentage error of a simulation done per each feature. Latency refers to the amount of past input data required to calculate the feature.

Scheirer and Slaney [65] have evaluated their models using 20 minutes long data sets of music and audio. Their data set consists of 80 samples, each with 15-second-long audio. They collected their samples using a 16-bit monophonic FM tuner with a sampling rate of 22.05 kHz, from a variety of stations, with different content styles

Features	The 4 Hz Mod Energy	The Low Energy	The Roll off	The Roll off Var	Spec Centroid	Spec Centroid Var	The Spec Flux	Spec Flux Var	The ZCR	The Var of the ZC Rate	The Cepstrum Resid	Cepstrum Res Var	The Pulse Metric
Latencies	1 sec	1 sec	1 frame	1 sec	1 frame	1 sec	1 frame	1 sec	1 frame	1 sec	1 frame	1 sec	5 sec
Errors	12 +/−1.7%	14 +/ −3.6%	46 +/− 2.9%	20 +/− 6.4%	39 +/− 8.0%	14 +/− 3.7%	39 +/− 1.1%	5.9 +/− 1.9%	38 +/− 4.6%	18 +/− 4.8%	37 +/− 7.5%	22 +/− %5.7	18 +/− % 2.9

Table 7.
Latency and univariate discrimination performance for each feature [65].

and different noise levels, over a period of three days in the San Francisco Bay Area. They also claimed that they have audios from both male and female.

They also recorded samples of many types of music, like pop, jazz, salsa, country, classical, reggae, various sorts of rock, various non-Western styles [29, 65]. They also used several features in a spatial partitioning classifier. **Table 8** summarizes their results.

The features used in Best 8 are the plus the 4 Hz modulation, the variance features, the pulse metric, and the low-energy frame [80, 134]. In the Best 3, they used the pulse metric, the 4 Hz energy, and the variance of spectral flux. In the Fast 5, they used the 5 basic features. From results shown in **Table 8**, we conclude that it is not necessary to use all features in order to have a good classification, so in real time a good performance system may be found using only few features. A more detailed discussion can be found in [29, 65, 80, 134].

3.3 Algorithms in the time-frequency domain

3.3.1 Spectrogram (or sonogram)

The spectrogram is an example of time-frequency distribution and this method was found to be a good classical tool for analyzing audio signal [13, 19, 86, 127]. The spectrogram (or sonogram) of a signal $x(n)$ can be defined as follow.

$$X(n,\omega) = \sum_{m=-N}^{N} W(n+m)x(m)e^{-j\omega\, m} \tag{26}$$

where N is the length of the sequence $x(n)$, and $W(n)$ is a specific window.

The method of spectrogram can be used in discriminating audio from music signal, however, it may have a high percentage error. That is because it depends on the strength of the frequency in the tested samples. **Figure 17** depicts two examples of spectrograms of audio and music signals.

3.3.2 Evolutionary spectrum (ES)

The spectral representation of a stationary signal may be viewed as an infinite sum of sinusoids with random amplitudes and phases as described in Eq. (27).

$$e(n) = \int_{-\pi}^{\pi} e^{j\omega n} dZ(\omega) \tag{27}$$

where $Z(\omega)$ is the process with orthogonal increments i.e.

$$E\{dZ^*(\omega)dZ(\Omega)\} = \frac{S(\omega)d\omega}{2\pi}\delta(\omega - \Omega) \tag{28}$$

Subset	All features	Best 8	Best 3	VS Flux only	Fast 5
Audio % Error	5.8 +/− 2.1	6.2 +/− 2.2	6.7 +/− 1.9	12 +/− 2.2	33 +/− 4.7
Music % Error	7.8 +/− 6.4	7.3 +/− 6.1	4.9 +/− 3.7	15 +/− 6.4	21 +/− 6.6
Total % Error	6.8 +/− 3.5	6.7 +/− 3.3	5.8 +/− 2.1	13 +/− 3.5	27 +/− 4.6

Table 8.
Performance for various subsets of features.

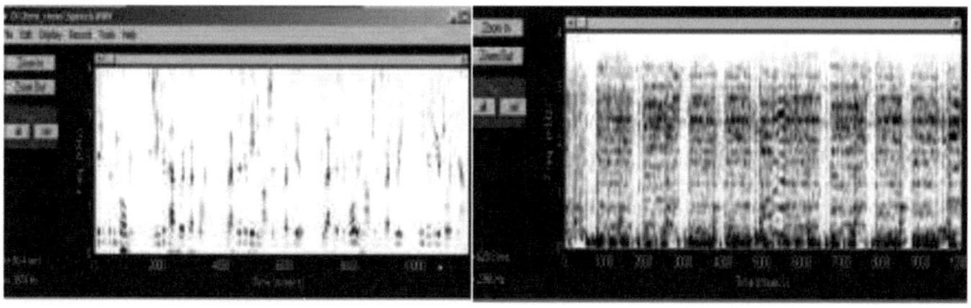

(a) (b)

Figure 17.
(a) Audio spectrogram, (b) music Spectrum.

and$S(\omega)$ in Eq. (28) is the spectrum of $e(n)$ [81]. Since the audio signal is, in general nonstationary, we will use the Wold-Cramer (WC) representation of a nonstationary signal. WC considers the discrete-time non-stationary process $\{x(n)\}$ as the output of a casual, linear, and time-variant (LTV) system with a white noise input $e(n)$ that has a zero-mean, unit-variant, i.e.,

$$x(n) = \sum_{m=\infty}^{n} h(n,m)e(n-m) \tag{29}$$

where $h(n,m)$ is defined as the unit impulse response of an LTV system. Substituting $e(n)$ into $x(n)$ of Eq. (29) (assuming $S(\omega)$ = 1 for white noise) we get.

$$x(n) = \int_{-\pi}^{\pi} H(n,\omega)e^{j\omega\, n}dZ(\omega) \tag{30}$$

where $H(n,\omega)$ in Eq. (30) is the time-frequency transfer function of the LTV system defined as

$$H(n,\omega) = \sum_{m=-\infty}^{n} h(n,m)e^{-j\omega\, m} \tag{31}$$

and the instantaneous power of $x(n)$ is given by

$$E\left\{|x(n)|^2\right\} = \frac{1}{2\pi}\int_{-\pi}^{\pi} |H(n,\omega)|^2 d\omega \tag{32}$$

and then, the Wold-Cramer ES is defined as

$$S(n,\omega) = \frac{1}{2\pi}|H(n,\omega)|^2 \tag{33}$$

The ES $S(n,\omega)$ in Eq. (33) was found to be a good classifier for the distinction of audio from music signals [81, 129]. Because of the extensive math calculation of the time-frequency spectrum, they may be very useful in off-line classification and analysis. The ESs of music and audio signals are shown in **Figure 18(a)** and **(b)**, respectively. The suppression of the amplitude for audio might due to gaussianity.

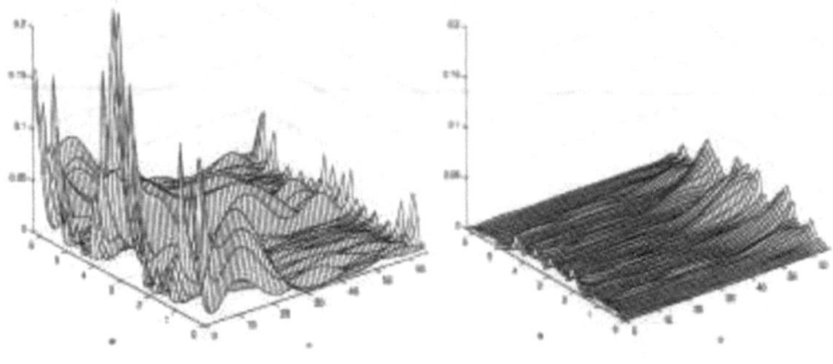

(a) (b)

Figure 18.
(a) The ES of a music signal, (b) the ES of an audio signal [81].

4. Separation of audio and music signals

Since the separation of audio and music signals is more complicated than classification, in this section we will introduce only two approaches [7–13, 22, 76, 77, 86, 135]. The first approach is the approach of independent component analysis (ICA) with ANN. The second classifier is the pitch cancelation approach. A block diagram of a classifier integrated with a separator is depicted in **Figure 19**.

4.1 ICA with ANN separation approach

In [13, 20, 21, 127, 136], Wang and Brown proposed a model for audio segregation algorithm. His model consists of preprocessing using cochlear filtering, gammatone filtering, and correlogram forming autocorrelation function and feature extraction. The impulse response of the gammatone filters is represented as.

$$h_i(t) = t^{n-1} e^{[(-2\pi b_i t)\ \cos\left(2\pi f_i t + \varphi_i\right)]}\, U(t)\, g(i), l \le i \le N \tag{34}$$

where n is the filter order, N is the number of channels, and U is the unit step function. Therefore, the gammatone system can be considered as a causal, time invariant system with an infinite response time. For the ith channel, fi is the center

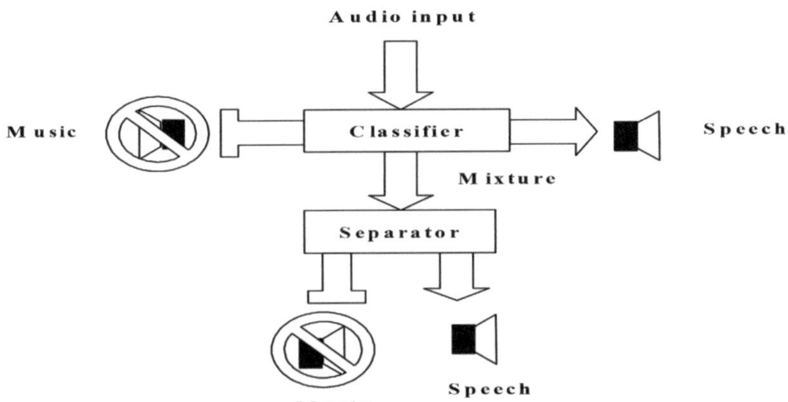

Figure 19.
A block diagram of a classifier integrated with a separator.

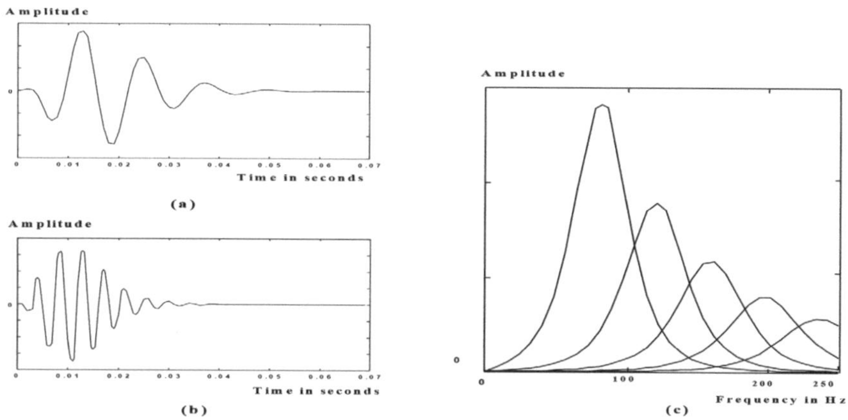

Figure 20.
4th order impulse response Gammatone system: (a) In time domain when i = 1, fi = 80 *Hz. (b) In time domain when* i = 5, fi = 244 *Hz. (c) In the frequency domain for the 1st five filters (i.e* i = 1 *to* i = 5*) with gain* g(i) *set to unity.*

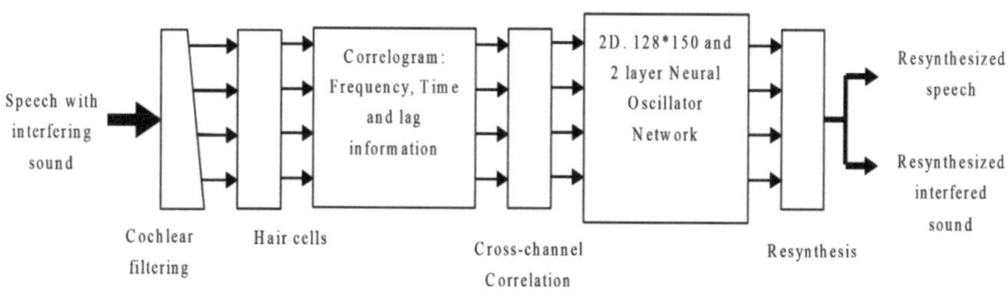

Figure 21.
A block diagram of Wang and Brown model.

frequency of the channel, ϕi is the phase of the channel, b is the rate of decay of the impulse response and $g(i)$ is an equalizing gain adjust for each filter. **Figure 20** depicts the impulse response of the gammatone system, where **Figure 21** depicts the block diagram of the Wang and Brown model.

Wang and Brown model has some drawbacks. The first drawback is its complexity. Their model needs a high specification hardware to perform the calculations. In [20], Andre reported that Wang and Brown model needs to be improved. The ICA method can be used for separation if two sources of mixture are available assuming that the two signals from the two different sources are statistically independent [66, 74, 75, 121, 137]. In [19], Takigawa tried to improve the performance of W & B model. He used the short time Fourier transform (STFT) in the input stage and used the spectrogram values instead of correlogram, however, they have not reported the amount of improvement. A similar work for separating the voiced audio of two talkers speaking simultaneously at similar intensities in a single channel, using pitch peak canceling in cepstrum domain, was done by Stubbs [8].

4.2 The pitch cancelation

The pitch cancelation method is widely used in noise reduction. A good try to separate two talkers speaking simultaneously at similar intensities in a single channel, or by other words, separation of two talkers without any restriction was introduced by Stubbs [8]. For a certain person, the letters A and R have lot of consonant. These consonants, in the frequency domain, have low amplitudes, however, they appear as long pitch peak in the cepstrum domain. If these consonants are deleted

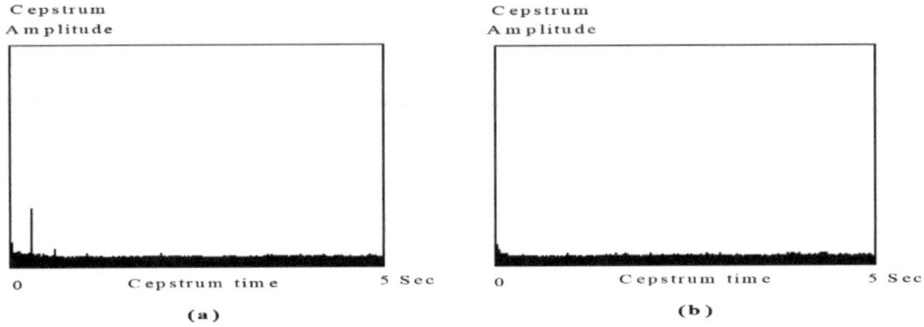

Figure 22.
(a) A typical 5 seconds audio signal in cepstrum domain, the pitch peak appears near zero. (b) a typical 5 seconds music signal in cepstrum domain.

by replacing the five-cepstral samples centered at the pitch peak by zeros, the audio segment may be attenuated or distorted completely. A typical example of the cepstrum of two audio and music signals is depicted in **Figure 22** for 5 seconds signals. The logarithmic effect will increase low amplitude reduce high one, and the values near zero will be very large after the logarithm.

5. Conclusions

In this chapter, a general review of the common classification and separation algorithms used for speech and music was presented and some were introduced and discussed thoroughly. The approaches dealt with classification were divided into three categories. The first category included most of the real-time approaches. In the real-time approaches, we introduced the ZCR, the STE, the ZCR and the STE with positive derivative, with some of their modified versions, and the neural networks. The second category included most of the frequency domain approaches such as the spectral centroid and its variance, the spectral flux and its variance, the roll-off of the spectrum, the cepstral residual, and the delta pitch. However, the last category introduced two time-frequency approaches, mainly the spectrogram and the evolutionary spectrum. It has been noticed that the time-frequency classifiers provided an excellent and a robust discrimination result in discriminating speech from music signals in digital audio. Depending on the application, the decision of which feature should be chosen is selected. The algorithms of the first category are faster since the processing is made in the real time; however, those of the second

Approaches	Time domain	Frequency domain (Spectrum) | (Cepstrum)		Time-Frequency domain
Algorithms	ZCR	Spectral Centroid	Cepstral Residual	Spectrogram (Sonogram)
	STE	Spectral Flux	Variance of the Cepstral Residual	Evolutionary Spectrum
	Roll-Off Variance	Spectrum Roll-Off	Cepstral feature	Evolutionary Bispectrum
	Pulse Metric	Signal Bandwidth	Pitch	
	Number of Silence	Spectrum Amplitude	Delta Pitch	
	HMM	Delta Amplitude		
	ANN			

Table 9.
Summary of the classification and separation algorithms.

one are more precise. The time-frequency approaches has not been discussed thoroughly in literature and they still need more research and elaboration. Lastly, we may conclude that many classification algorithms were proposed in literature, however, few ones were proposed for separation. The algorithms introduced in this chapter can be summarized in **Table 9**.

Author details

Abdullah I. Al-Shoshan
Computer Engineering, Qassim University, Saudi Arabia

*Address all correspondence to: ashoshan@qu.edu.sa

References

[1] Al-Shoshan A. I. Speech and Music Classification and Separation: A Review. Journal of King Saud University-Engineering Sciences. 2006; 19(1): 95–133. doi:10.1016/S1018-3639(18)30850-X

[2] Martin, K. Towards Automatic Sound Source Recognition: Identifying Musical Instruments. In: Proceedings of NATO Computational Hearing Advanced Study Institute, Italy, July 1998.

[3] Herrera-Boyer P., Amatriain X., Batlle E., Serra X. Towards Instrument Segmentation for Music Content Description: a Critical Review of Instrument Classification Techniques. In: Proceedings of International Society for Music Information Retrieval (ISMIR), 2000.

[4] Gjerdingen R.O. Using Connectionist Models to Explore Complex Musical Patterns. Computer Music Journal. 1989; 13(3):67–75. DOI: 10.2307/3680013

[5] Hörnel D., Menzel W. Learning Musical Structure and Style with Neural Networks. Computer Music Journal. 1998; 22(4):44–62. doi:10.2307/3680893

[6] Leman, M., Van Renterghem P. Transputer Implementation of the Kohonen Feature Map for a Music Recognition Task. In: Proceedings of the Second International Transputer Conference; Antwerpen: BIRA, 1989. pp. 1–20

[7] Al-Atiyah A. Music and Speech Separation [thesis]. King Saud University; 2002.

[8] Stubbs R., Summerfield Q. Effects of signal-to-noise ratio, signal periodicity, and degree of hearing impairment on the performance of voice-separation algorithms. J. Acoustical Society of America. 1991; 89:1383–1393. DOI: 10.1121/1.400539

[9] Lee T-W., Koehler B-U. Blind Source Separation of Nonlinear Mixing Modes. In: Proceedings of the IEEE Signal Processing Society Workshop (1997). Amelia Island, FL. USA: IEEE; 1997. pp. 406–415. doi: 10.1109/NNSP.1997.622422

[10] Lee T-W., Orglmeister R. A Contextual Blind Separation of Delayed and Convolved Sources. IEEE ICASSP'97; (1997). pp. 1199–1202. DOI: 10.1109/ICASSP.1997.596159

[11] Lee T-W., Bell A., Lambert R. Blind Separation of Convolved and Delayed Sources. Advance in Neural Information Processing System. MIT Press. 1997.

[12] Lee T-W., Bell A. J., Orglmeister R. Blind Source Separation of Real Word Signals. IEEE ICNN. Houston, USA; (1997). 2129–2134. DOI: 10.1109/ICNN.1997.614235

[13] Wang D. L., Brown G. J. Separation of Speech From Interfering Sounds Based on Oscillatory Correlation. IEEE Transaction on Neural Networks. Vol. 10: No. 3. (May 1999), 684–697. DOI: 10.1109/72.761727

[14] Leman M. The Theory of Tone Semantics: Concept, Foundation, and Application, Minds and Machines. 2(4): (1992); pp. 345–363. doi.org/10.1007/BF00419418

[15] Patel A.D., Gibson E., Ratner J., Besson M., Holcomb P.J. Processing Grammatical Relations in Music and Language: An Event-Related Potential (ERP) Study. Proceedings of the Fourth International Conference on Music Perception and Cognition. Montreal: McGill University. (1996). 337–342.

[16] Stevens C., Latimer C. A Comparison of Connectionist Models of Music Recognition and Human

Performance. Minds and Machines, 2 (4): (1992); pp. 379–400.

[17] Weigend A.S. Connectionism for Music and Audition. In J. Cowan, G. Tesauro & J. Alspector (Eds.), Advances in Neural Information Processing Systems 6, San Francisco: Morgan Kaufmann. (1994); pp. 1163–1164.

[18] Anagnostopoulou C., Westermann G. Classification in Music: A Computational Model for Paradigmatic Analysis. Proceedings of the International Computer Music Conference, San Francisco, (1997), 125–128.

[19] Takigawa I., Toyama J., Shimbo M. A Modified LEGION using a spectrogram for speech segregation. IEEE. (1999); I526-I531. DOI: 10.1109/ICSMC.1999.814147

[20] Andre J. W., Kouwe V. D., Wang D., Brown G. J. A Comparison of Auditory and blind Separation Techniques for speech segregation. IEEE transaction on speech and audio processing. 9(3): (March 2001); pp. 189–195. DOI: 10.1109/89.905993

[21] Wang D. L., Brown G. J. Speech Segregation on Sound Localization. IEEE, (2001), 2861–2866.

[22] Belouchrani A., Aben-Meraim K., Cardoso J. F., Moulines E. A Blind Source Separation Technique Using Second Order Statistics. IEEE Trans. Signal processing, vol. 45, (Feb. 1997), pp. 434–444. DOI: 10.1109/78.554307

[23] Govindarajan K.K., Grossberg S., Wyse L.L., Cohen M.A. A Neural Network Model of Auditory Scene Analysis and Source Segregation. Technical Report CAS/CNS-TR-94-039, Boston University, Dept. of Cognitive and Neural Systems, 1994.

[24] Kahrs M., Brandenburg K. Application of digital signal processing to audio and acoustics. Kluwer Academic Puplisher, Bosten/ Dordrecht/ London, 1998.

[25] Backus J. The Acoustical Foundations of Music. 2nd, W. W. Norton & Company, 1977.

[26] Gang D., Lehmann D., Wagner N. Harmonizing Melodies in Real-Time: The Connectionist Approach. Proceedings of the International Computer Music Conference, San Francisco, (1997), pp. 27–31.

[27] Kaipainen M., Toiviainen P., Louhivuori J. A Self-Organizing Map that Recognizes and Generates Melodies. In P. Pylkkänen & P. Pylkkö (Eds.), New Directions in Cognitive Science, (1995), 286–315.

[28] Port R., Anderson S. Recognition of Melody Fragments in Continuously Performed Music. Proceedings of the Eleventh Annual Conference of the Cognitive Science Society, Hillsdale, NJ: Erlbaum Associates, (1989), 820–827.

[29] Toiviainen P. Modeling the Target-Note Technique of Bebop-Style Jazz Improvisation: An Artificial Neural Network Approach. Music Perception, 12(4), (1995), 399–413.

[30] Cook, N. A Guide to Musical Analysis. Oxford University Press, 1987.

[31] Roy, D. and Malamud, C. Speaker Identification Based Text to Audio Alignment for an Audio Retrieval System. IEEE ICASSP'97, vol. 2, Munich, Germany, (April 1997), 1099–1102.

[32] Beigi H., Maes S., Sorensen J., Chaudhari U. A Hierarchical Approach to Large-Scale Speaker Recognition. IEEE ICASSP'99, Phoenix, Arizona, March 1999.

[33] Rabiner L., Juang B. H. Fundamentals of Speech Recognition.

Prentice-Hall, Englewood Cliffs, NJ, 1993.

[34] Kedem B. Spectral Analysis and Discrimination by Zero-Crossings. Proceedings of IEEE, Vol. 74, NO. 11, (Nov. 1986), 1477–1492.

[35] Bateman W. Introduction to Computer Music. John Wiley&sons, 1984.

[36] Fedor P. Principles of the Design of D-Neuronal Networks I: Net Representation for Computer Simulation of a Melody Compositional Process. International Journal of Neural Systems, 3(1), (1992), 65–73.

[37] Horner A., Goldberg D.E. Genetic Algorithms and Computer-Assisted Music Composition. In B. Alphonce & B. Pennycock (Eds.), Proceedings of the 1991 International Computer Music Conference, San Francisco, (1991), 479–482.

[38] McIlwain P. The Yuri Program: Computer Generated Music for Multi-Speaker Sound Systems. Proceedings of the ACMA Conference, Melbourne, Australia, (1995), 150–151.

[39] Ainsworth W. A. Speech Recognition by Machine. Peter Peregrinus Ltd., 1988.

[40] Muthusamy Y. K., Barnard E., Cole R. A. Reviewing Automatic Language Identification. IEEE Signal Processing Magazine, (October 1994), 33–41.

[41] Ladefoged P. Elements of Acoustic Phonetics. University of Chicago Press, 1962.

[42] Fry D. B. The Physics of Speech. Cambridge University Press, 1979.

[43] Beck D.L., Callaway S.L. Breakthroughs in signal processing and feedback reduction lead to better speech understanding. Hearing Review. 2019; 26(4) [Apr]:30–31.

[44] Linster C. Rhythm Analysis with Backpropagation. In R. Pfeifer, Z. Schreter, F. Fogelman-Soulie & L. Steels (Eds.), Connectionism in Perspective, North-Holland: Elsevier Science Publishers B.V, (1989), 385–393.

[45] Jakobsson M. Machine-Generated Music with Themes. Proceedings of the International Conference on Artificial Neural Networks (Vol. 2) Amsterdam: Elsevier, (1992), 1645–1646.

[46] Griffith N.J.L. Connectionist Visualization of Tonal Structure. AI Review, 8, (1995), 393–408.

[47] Stevens C., Wiles J. Representations of Tonal Music: A Case Study in the Development of Temporal Relationships. In M.C. Mozer, P. Smolensky, D.S. Touretzky, J.E. Elman & A.S. Weigend (Eds.), Proceedings of the Connectionist Models Summer School, Hillsdale, NJ: Erlbaum, (1993), 228–235.

[48] Young P. H. Electrical Communication Techniques. 2nd, MERRILL, 1990.

[49] Laine P. Generating Musical Patterns Using Mutually Inhibited Artificial Neurons. Proceedings of the International Computer Music Conference, San Francisco, (1997), 422–425.

[50] Leman M. Symbolic and Subsymbolic Description of Music. In G. Haus (Ed.), Music Processing, New York: Oxford University Press, (1993), 119–164.

[51] Lischka C. Understanding Music Cognition: A Connectionist View. In G. De Poli, A. Piccialli & C. Roads (Eds.), Representations of Musical Signals, Cambridge, MA: MIT Press, (1991), 417–445.

[52] Griffith N., Todd P. M. Musical Networks. Bradford Books The MIT Press, 1999.

[53] Pierce J. R. The Science of Musical Sound. 3rd Ed., W.H.Freeman and company, 1996.

[54] Lerdahl F. and Jackendoff, R., A Generative Theory of Tonal Music. MIT Press, Cambridge, 1983.

[55] Monelle R. Linguistics and Semiotics in Music. Harwood Academic Publishers, 1992.

[56] Gang D., Berger J. Modeling the Degree of Realized Expectation in Functional Tonal Music: A Study of Perceptual and Cognitive Modeling Using Neural Networks. In D. Rossiter (Ed.), Proceedings of the International Computer Music Conference, San Francisco, (1996), 454–457.

[57] Bharucha J. Tonality and Expectation. In R. Aiello (Ed.), Musical Perceptions, New York: Oxford University Press, (1994), 213–239.

[58] Feiten B., Ungvary T. "Organizing Sounds with Neural Nets", Int. Computer Music Conference, San Francisco, (1991), 441–443.

[59] Foote J. T. Content-Based Retrieval of Music and Audio. SPIE'97, (1997), 138–147.

[60] Saunders J. Real-Time Discrimination of Broadcast Speech/ Music. IEEE ICASSP'96, (1996), 993–996.

[61] El-maleh K., Samoulian A., Kabal P. Frame-Level Noise Classification in Mobile Environment. proc. IEEE Int. Conf. On Acoustics, Speech, Signal processing, Phoenix, Arizona, (March 1999), 237–240.

[62] El-maleh K., Klein M., Petrucci G., Kabal P. Speech/Music Discriminator for Multimedia Application. Proc. IEEE Int. Conf. Acoustics, Speech, Signal Processing (Istanbul), (June 2000), 2445–2448.

[63] Benyamin M., Miriam F. Neural Network Based Model for Classification of Music Type. IEEE Cat., No. 95, (1995), 640–645.

[64] Hoyt J. D., Wechsler H. Detection of Human Speech Using Hybrid Recognition Models. IEEE, (1994), 330–333.

[65] Scheirer E., Slaney M. Construction and Evaluation of a Robust Multifeature Speech/Music Discriminator. Proceedings of the 1997 International Conference on Acoustics, Speech, and Signal Processing (ICASSP97), Munich, Germany, April 1997.

[66] Chien J-T. Source Separation and Machine Learning. Elsevier Inc. 2019. https://doi.org/10.1016/C2015-0-02300-0

[67] Pope S. T., Holm F., Kouznetsov A. Feature extraction and database design for music software. Proceedings of the International Computer Music Conference, (2004), 596–603.

[68] McKay C., Fujinaga I. Automatic genre classification using large high-level musical feature sets, Proceedings of the International Conference on Music Information Retrieval, (2004), 525–530.

[69] Essed S., Richard G., David B. Musical instrument recognition based on class pairwise feature selection. Proceedings of the International Conference on Music Information Retrieval, (2004), 560–568.

[70] Downie J. The scientific evaluation of music information retrieval systems: Foundations and future. Computer Music Journal, 28, 2, (2004), 12–33.

[71] West K., Cox, S. Finding an Optimal Segmentation for Audio Genre

Classification. Proceedings of the 6th Int. Symposium on Music Information Retrieval, University of London, (2005), 680–685.

[72] Tzanetaki G. Music Information Retrieval. ICASSP2005, Tutorial TUT-5, Philadelphia, 2005.

[73] West C., Cox S. Features and classifiers for the automatic classification of musical audio signals. Proceedings of the International Conference on Music Information Retrieval, (2004), 531–537.

[74] Yang X-S. Introduction to Algorithms for Data Mining and Machine Learning. Elsevier Inc. 2019. https://doi.org/10.1016/C2018-0-02034-4

[75] Kotu V. Data Science: Concepts and Practice. Elsevier Inc. 2019. https://doi.org/10.1016/C2017-0-02113-4

[76] Mimilakis S. I., Drossos K., Cano E. Schuller G. Examining the Mapping Functions of Denoising Autoencoders in Singing Voice Separation. IEEE/ACM Transactions on Audio, Speech, and Language Processing. vol. 28, pp. 266–278, 2020. DOI: 10.1109/TASLP.2019.2952013

[77] Sharma G., Umapathy K., Krishnan S. Trends in audio signal feature extraction methods. Applied Acoustics. Elsevier Ltd. Volume 158, 15 January 2020. https://doi.org/10.1016/j.apacoust.2019.107020

[78] Al-Shoshan A., Al-Atiyah A., Al-Mashouq K. A Three-Level Speech, Music, and Mixture Classifier. Journal of King Saud University {Engineering Sciences (No. 2)}, Volume 16, (1424), 319–332. https://doi.org/10.1016/S1018-3639(18)30794-3

[79] Al-Shoshan, A.I., "A Classification of Music, Speech and Mixture Signals Via Fuzzy Logic," The 28th International Conference on Computers and Their Applications, (CATA-2013), Honolulu, Hawaii, USA, pp. 117–122, March 4–6, 2013.

[80] Berger J., Gang D. A Neural Network Model of Metric Perception and Cognition in the Audition of Functional Tonal Music. Proceedings of the 1997 International Computer Music Conference, San Francisco, (1997), 23–26.

[81] Al-Shoshan, A.I., "Audio Signal Discrimination Using Evolutionary Spectrum," International Journal of Computers and Applications, Volume 31, No. 2, pp. 69–73, 2009.

[82] Toiviainen P., Kaipainen M., Louhivuori J. Musical Timbre: Similarity Ratings Correlate with Computational Feature Space Distances. Journal of New Music Research, 24(3), (1995), 282–298.

[83] Jin H., Kubala F., Schwartz R. Automatic Speaker Clustering. Proc. of the Speech Recognition Workshop, (1997), 108–111.

[84] Meddis R., Hewitt M. Modeling the Identification of Concurrent Vowels with Different Fundamental Frequency. J. Acoust. Soc. Am., vol. 91, (1992), 233–245.

[85] Raphael C. "Automatic Segmentation of Acoustic Musical Signals Using Hidden Markov Models", IEEE Transactions on Pattern Analysis and Machine Intelligence, vol.21, No. 4, April 1999.

[86] Hyvarinen, A. and Oja, E. Independent Component Analysis: Algorithms and Applications. Int. J. of Neural Networks, April 1999.

[87] Akarte N.J. Music Composition Using Neural Networks. Master's thesis, University of Nevada, Reno, 1992.

[88] Barnard E., Cole R.A., Vea M.P., Alleva F.A. Pitch Detection with a Neural-Net Classifier. IEEE

Transactions on Signal Processing, 39 (2), (1991), 298–307.

[89] Bellgard M.I., Tsang C.P. Harmonizing Music Using a Network of Boltzmann Machines. In Proceedings of the Fifth Annual Conference of Artificial Neural Networks and Their Applications (Neuro-Nimes), (1992), 321–332.

[90] Bellgard M.I., Tsang C.P. "On the use of an Effective Boltzmann Machine for Musical Style Recognition and Harmonization", Proceedings of the International Computer Music Conference, San Francisco, (1996), 461–464.

[91] Berger J., Gang D. Modeling Musical Expectations: A Neural Network Model of Dynamic Changes of Expectation in the Audition of Functional Tonal Music. Proceedings of the Fourth International Conference on Music Perception and Cognition, Montreal: McGill University, (1996), 373–378.

[92] Bharucha J. Neural Net Modeling of Music. Proceedings of the First Workshop on Artificial Intelligence and Music, Menlo Park, CA, (1988), 173–182.

[93] Bharucha J. Neural Networks and Perceptual Learning of Tonal Expectancies. Proceedings of the First International Conference on Music Perception and Cognition, Kyoto: Kyoto City University of Arts, (1989), 81–86.

[94] Bharucha J. Pitch, Harmony and Neural Nets: A Psychological Perspective. In P.M. Todd & D.G. Loy (Eds.), Music and Connectionism, Cambridge, MA: MIT Press, (1991), 84–99.

[95] Bharucha J., Olney K.L. Tonal Cognition, Artificial Intelligence and Neural Nets. Contemporary Music Review, Vol. 4, (1989), 341–356.

[96] Bresin R, Vedovetto A. Neural Networks for Musical Tones Compression, Control, and Synthesis. In Proceedings of the International Computer Music Conference, San Francisco, (1994), 368–371.

[97] Bresin R., Vedovetto A. Neural Networks for the Compression of Musical Tones and for the Control of Their Resynthesis. Proceedings of the IEEE-SP International Symposium on Time-Frequency and Time-Scale Analysis, 1994.

[98] Carpinteiro O. A Neural Model to Segment Musical Pieces. In E. Miranda (Ed.), Proceedings of the Second Brazilian Symposium on Computer Music, Fifteenth Congress of the Brazilian Computer Society, (1995), 114–120.

[99] Ciaccia P., Lugli F., Maio D. Using Neural Networks to Perform Harmonic Analysis in Music. The Fifth Italian Workshop on Neural Nets, WIRN VIETRI-92, Singapore, (1992), 273–279.

[100] Cosi P., DePoli G., Lauzzana G. Auditory Modeling and Self-Organizing Neural Networks for Timbre Classification. Journal of New Music Research, 23(1), (1994), 71–98.

[101] Fedor P. Principles of the Design of D-Neuronal Networks II: Composing Simple Melodies. International Journal of Neural Systems, 3(1), (1992), 75–82.

[102] Feiten B., Guenzel S. Automatic Indexing of a Sound Data Base Using Self-Organizing Neural Nets. Computer Music Journal, 18(3), (1994), 53–65.

[103] Feulner J. Learning the Harmonies of Western Tonal Music Using Neural Networks. Proceedings of the International Symposium on Computer and Information Sciences VII, Paris: EHEI Press, (1992), 303–307.

[104] Feulner J. Neural Networks that Learn and Reproduce Various Styles of Harmonization. Proceedings of the

International Computer Music Conference, San Francisco, (1993), 236–239.

[105] Gang D., Lehmann D. An Artificial Neural Net for Harmonizing Melodies. Proceedings of the International Computer Music Conference, San Francisco, (1995), 440–447.

[106] Gjerdingen R.O. Categorization of Musical Patterns by Self-Organizing Neuronlike Networks. Music Perception, 7(4), (1990), 339–370.

[107] Laden B. A Parallel Learning Model for Pitch Perception. Journal of New Music Research, 23(2), (1994), 133–144.

[108] Laden B., Keefe B.H. The Representation of Pitch in a Neural Net Model of Pitch Classification. Computer Music Journal, 13(4), (1989), 12–26. Also in P.M. Todd & D.G. Loy (Eds.), Music and Connectionism, Cambridge, MA: MIT Press, (1991), 64–78.

[109] Leman M. Artificial Neural Networks in Music Research. In A. Marsden & A. Pople (Eds.), Computer Representations and Models in Music, London: Academic Press, (1991), 265–301.

[110] Mencl W.E. Effects of Tuning Sharpness on Tone Categorization by Self-Organizing Neural Networks. Proceedings of the Fourth International Conference on Music Perception and Cognition, Montreal: McGill University, (1996), 217–218.

[111] Mourjopoulos J.N., Tsoukalas D.E. Neural Network Mapping to Subjective Spectra of Music Sounds. Journal of the Audio Engineering Society, 40(4), (1992), 253–259.

[112] Cohen M.A., Grossberg S., Wyse L.L. A Spectral Network Model of Pitch Perception. Journal of the Acoustical Society of America, 498(2), (1995), 862–879. https://doi.org/10.1121/1.413512.

[113] Ohya K. A Sound Synthesis by Recurrent Neural Network. In E. Michie (Ed.), Proceedings of the International Computer Music Conference, San Francisco, (1995), 420–423.

[114] Palmieri F. Learning Binaural Sound Localization through a Neural Network, Proceedings of the IEEE Seventeenth Annual Northeast Bioengineering Conference, (1991), 13–14.

[115] Röbel A. Neural Networks for Modeling Time Series of Musical Instruments. In E. Michie (Ed.), Proceedings of the International Computer Music Conference, San Francisco, (1995), 424–428.

[116] Röbel A. Neural Network Modeling of Speech and Music Signals. In M.C. Mozer, M.I. Jordan & T. Petsche (Eds.), Advances in Neural Information Processing Systems 9, Cambridge, MA: MIT Press, 1997.

[117] Sano H., Jenkins K.B. A Neural Network Model for Pitch Perception. Computer Music Journal, 13(3), (1989), 41–48. Also in P.M. Todd & D.G. Loy (Eds.), Music and Connectionism, Cambridge, MA: MIT Press, (1991), 42–49.

[118] Taylor I. Artificial Neural Network Types for the Determination of Musical Pitch. Unpublished doctoral thesis, University of Wales, College of Cardiff, Dept. of Physics, 1994.

[119] Taylor I. J. Greenhough, M. Neural Network Pitch Tracking Over the Pitch Continuum. In E. Michie (Ed.), Proceedings of the International Computer Music Conference, San Francisco, (1995), 432–435.

[120] Trubitt D.R., Todd P.M. The Computer Musician: Neural Networks and Computer Music. Electronic Musician, 7(1), (1991), 20–24.

[121] Walpole R. E., Myers R. H. Probability and Statistics for Engineer

and Scientists. 5th Ed., Macmillan Publishing, 1993.

[122] Bogert B. P., Healy M. J. R., Tukey J. W. The Quefrency Alanysis of Time Series for Echoes: Cepstrum, Pseudo-autocovariance, Cross-Cepstrum, and Saphe Cracking. John Wiley and Sons, New York, (1963), 209–243.

[123] Eronen A., Klapuri A. Musical Instrument Recognition using cepstral coefficients and temporal features", Proc. ICASSP 2000.

[124] Cosi P., DePoli G., Prandoni P. "Timbre characterization with mel-cepstrum and neural nets", Proceedings of the International Computer Music Conference, (1994), 42–45.

[125] Griffith N. J. L. Modeling the Influence of Pitch Duration on the Induction of Tonality from Pitch-use. Proceedings of the International Computer Music Conference, San Francisco, (1994), 35–37.

[126] Taylor I., Greenhough M. An Object Oriented ARTMAP System for Classifying Pitch. Proceedings of the International Computer Music Conference, San Francisco, (1993), 244–247.

[127] Mu G., Wang D. L. An Extended Model for Speech Segregation. Proceeding of IEEE, (2001), 1089–1094.

[128] Priestley M. B. Non-linear and Non-stationary Time Series Analysis. New York, NY:Academic Press, 1988.

[129] Al-Shoshan A.I. LTV System Identification Using the Time-Varying Autocorrelation Function and Application to Audio Signal Discrimination. ICSP02, Bejing, China, 2002. DOI: 10.1109/ICOSP.2002.1181036

[130] Scarborough D.L., Miller B.O., Jones, J.A. Connectionist Models for Tonal Analysis. Computer Music Journal, 13(3), (1989), 49–55. Also in P. M. Todd & D.G. Loy (Eds.), Music and Connectionism, Cambridge, MA: MIT Press, (1991), 54–60.

[131] Shuttleworth T., Wilson R., A Neural Network for Triad Classification. In E. Michie (Ed.), Proceedings of the International Computer Music Conference, San Francisco, (1995), 428–431.

[132] Sergent J. Mapping the Musician Brain, Human Brain Mapping, (1993), 20–38.

[133] Rossignol S., Rodet X., Soumagne J., Collette L., Depalle P. Feature extraction and temporal segmentation of acoustic signals. Proceedings of the International Computer Music Conference, 1998.

[134] Scarborough D.L., Miller B.O., Jones J.A. On the Perception of Meter. In M. Balaban, K. Ebcioglu & O. Laske (Eds.), Understanding Music with AI: Perspectives in Music Cognition, Cambridge, MA: MIT Press, (1992), 427–447.

[135] Magron P., Virtanen T. Online Spectrogram Inversion for Low-Latency Audio Source Separation. IEEE Signal Processing Letters. vol. 27, pp. 306–310, 2020. DOI: 10.1109/LSP.2020.2970310

[136] Wang D. L. Primitive Auditory Segregation Based on Oscillator Correlation. Cognit. Sci., vol. 20, (1996), 409–456.

[137] Israr M., Khan M. S., Khan K. Speech Sources Separation Based on Models of Interaural Parameters and Spatial Properties of Room. International Journal of Engineering Works. 7(1): January 2020; pp. 22–26. https://doi.org/10.34259/ijew.20.7012226